THE WORLD
IN MY BONES

THE WORLD IN MY BONES

The Diplomat Queens Made

JENNIFER ERIE

First Edition

Editor: Maria MacAndrew

ISBN: 9798994259900

DEDICATION

To God, the one who saw me before I saw myself and who orders my steps even when I don't understand the path. Thank you.

And to my late beloved mother, Ginette, whose prayers covered me, whose sacrifices anchored me, and whose love continues to light my way.

You were good enough, and your spirit lives on in every chapter of my life. This story is as much yours as it is mine.

Mesi anpil.

I love you.

TABLE OF CONTENTS

FOREWORD

It is my absolute honor to pen the foreword for Jennifer Erie's remarkable memoir, a story that spans continents, cultures, and the resilient spirit of possibility. Our first meeting still fills me with pride: Black History Month at John Snow, Inc. (JSI) in Virginia, a gathering that celebrated not just the triumphs of Black Americans but also the global bonds forged when paths cross in unlikely places. Thanks to our steadfast mutual friend, Colonel (Ret.) Vance Shaw, I met a young woman brimming with purpose and questions, who would soon chart her own course through public service.

What struck me about Jennifer from that initial conversation was her tenacity and sincere curiosity about international affairs. She reminded me of the hunger I felt as a young man growing up in St. Albans, Queens, where opportunity was hard-earned, and our parents exhorted us to make spaces for ourselves where none seemed to exist. That day, rather than limit her to pleasantries, I invited Jennifer to the State Department. I wanted to offer the kind of access and insight that senior officers, including the late Ambassador Ruth A. Davis and C. Stephen McGann, provided me.

My decision to introduce Jennifer to Alonzo Fulgham was not taken lightly. Alonzo was a respected leader at USAID, and I knew he would value only a recommendation with substance. I quickly recognized the promise in Jennifer's approach: her questions had depth, and her ambitions were firmly rooted in a desire to serve the public good. When I later served as Ambassador in Manila, her first post with USAID, I had a front-row seat to watch Jennifer's growth from a driven officer navigating a new world to a leader who earned the trust and respect of her colleagues.

In Jennifer's journey, I see the echo of my own: two Queens kids, raised in working-class neighborhoods—St. Albans for me, Laurelton and Hollis for her—where the dreams of diplomacy seemed, at one time, worlds away from our streets. Statistically, the odds were against us, but history favors those who persist. Jennifer has consistently shown the courage to enter spaces not built for her and to help expand them for those who come after.

Jennifer's story is not just hers. It is a beacon for young people in every working-class city, a reminder that their aspirations are valid and possible. I hope that as you read this book, you will be inspired not only by her accomplishments but by the deep well of integrity, resilience, and hope from which she draws.

— Harry K. Thomas, Jr.
U.S. Ambassador (Retired)

Introduction

BEFORE I BEGIN, LET ME BE HONEST

I am sitting on the marble top of my mother's bench-gravestone, legs overlapping the way I used to cross them in embassy conference rooms. I am in pain, deep pain. The cold of the stone seeps through my jeans and settles deep in my bones, a familiar ache in my neck and hips. It mirrors the cold in my heart, a grief so sharp it feels similar to the fractures I have endured. And when I stand up from here, I pray I don't crack another joint because, God help me, I cannot afford another surgery. Not right now.

The grass is wet with dew. The early light, the color of weak tea, does nothing to warm me. My tote bag rests at my feet like a silent attaché. Inside, the diplomatic passport that once opened doors is now just a rectangle of stiff pages with two punched holes on the front flap. The USAID lapel pin I used to wear proudly sits in a small, vibrantly patterned *kitenge* pouch. I can still feel the thick cotton weave, a reminder of the markets where I found it.

Tucked beside the USAID lapel pin is a photograph of my son, Anthony, age seven, grinning in a Manila schoolyard, unaware that every boarding pass I clipped was carving his life's path in unconventional ways.

My bag also holds the final, one-line email from USAID:

Reduction-in-Force. Effective September 2. Separation date final.

I have returned to a country that no longer feels like home. This is not a retirement. I was not ready to stop working, to stop serving, or to start over. But here I am anyway, carrying a suitcase of memories, unfinished work, and the ache of endings I did not choose.

For over twenty-five years, I've worked and lived in other people's countries. I stamped "home" onto each place like a visa, willing the belonging into being. But what does it really mean to belong?

I still ask myself if I did the right thing, not just for me but for Anthony. He is twenty-two now, and he can easily measure friendship in good-byes. What was the price of this life for him? I can still hear the final taps of his basketball bouncing down a Pretoria driveway the day the moving truck came, and his voice reminding me that we were leaving behind yet another chapter in our storied journey.

That day, we had little to show for our time there. All we mainly carried were a few niche souvenirs and our clothes. Now, as I look at them, some of those trinkets are losing their luster. All I really carry is a passport full of pages and nowhere that currently feels like home. I hope to create a home once again. Hopefully, in the future, I will not always be "the other."

But why am I telling you all this and why now?

I am letting you into my life to show you the beauty, the joy, and the pain of several chapters I am now leaving behind. As I write this, I am back home in one sense, but with no home to go back to. I feel like an internally displaced person in America.

I crave my mother's kitchen. I miss the salt and heat of her *griot* and *banane peze*, or the *soup joumou* she prepared every January 1st. Without her, the celebration of Haitian Independence has lost its anchor. Home was never a house or a city; it was her. Now she lies under the rubble, directly beneath my feet. I thought I was out of tears, but they came anyway. I have no name for this feeling and no map for what comes next.

Here is what I know: tomorrow is another opportunity to do some good in the world. Anthony still thinks he's Lebron James when he scores a three-pointer at the neighborhood court. My mother's stone is warm now where the sun has found it, and I can come back tomorrow if I want, and the day after that.

I wonder where I will go next. Maybe I'll start in a classroom, showing kids a passport for the first time, or at conferences that need a voice that has slept under multiple different constellations. Maybe I will speak to entrepreneurs who think risk means launching a startup and need to hear what it looks like when it wears a bulletproof vest. Or maybe I'll take up a painting or photography class and create the art that lives in my heart and soul. I want to bring the world back home, to echo the Peace Corps' third goal and fight against various forms of injustice, whether in a classroom, a boardroom, on a canvas, or elsewhere.

What I can do is start right here, right now. I am giving myself permission to open my life to you. Walk with me through these pages.

This book is the moment I stop hiding the limp. It is the permission I give myself to sit on gravestones and cry in daylight, to laugh so hard the titanium creaks. It is the long exhale after holding my breath across continents. It is the beginning of my story of coming back to America and the end of the silence I kept while I was away. It is my personal freedom bursting outside of the boxes.

I wrote these pages because the weight I carried finally demanded to be named. For decades, I kept family and diplomatic secrets tucked behind a polite smile, believing silence was the price of respect. My mother took her stories to the grave; I will not take mine. Her death loosened the last knot, finally permitting me to speak without wounding her.

I also wrote this because I am tired of watching people believe their losses are the end of their story. In a single week, I lost my mother, my livelihood, and the illusion that any place is permanent. I wrote to prove that endings can be opening acts, that a diplomat can become a student again, and a woman who once stamped visas for others can finally stamp her own second chance.

This book is for anyone who has perfected the art of looking fine while falling apart. It is for the girl from Queens who learned to swallow her accent, and her fear in the same gulp, who discovered that silence could be currency. It is for the federal worker who received a two-line email that ended a career, and the single parent who packed boxes in the dark so her child could still believe that adventure outweighed loss.

It is for that 'around the way' teenager, standing at a subway turnstile with a MetroCard and no map, certain that leaving the neighborhood is betrayal and staying is surrender. I wrote this for the readers who refuse to believe their stories are too small, too messy, or too ordinary.

Most of all, I wrote it because healing rarely comes neatly wrapped with a bow. Real healing happens when you run your finger along the scar and decide it's still part of you.

If you have ever hidden a hurt because revealing it felt like one more burden, I offer you this book as evidence that telling your truth is lighter than carrying fear and shame.

I can promise honesty, a passport full of adventures, and the stubborn hope that what feels like breaking may be the sound of something opening.

Turn the page. Nothing is footnoted. Join me in this journey of transparent reflection, humility, and discovery. Enjoy the boldly colored jeepneys and epic karaoke in the Philippines; the magical rose-gold hush of sunsets over Zanzibar; beauty that left me breathless in South Sudan; food choices that defeated me in crowded Bangkok markets; and the unexpected joy of rebuilding a life, one day at a time.

Chapter One

WHAT HAPPENED TO PRINCESS?

D ad drove her all the way to Brooklyn and left her there so she wouldn't find her way back.

That's what my older sister Nancy told me recently about our dog, with a chuckle. And of course, I laughed too, because what else do you do with a memory like that?

I still see my four-year-old self with my face pressed against the chain-link fence, watching Princess. That memory remains a fixture of my early years. Princess was a beautiful German Shepherd with a fluffy golden coat, a gentle giant in our Queens backyard. I used to think our poor dog was a pony. I'd grab her collar and try to ride her around the house, which perfectly explains why she started disappearing the second she saw me coming.

Throughout my adulthood, I sometimes wondered what had ever happened to her. To hear that we dumped her far from home and left her to survive on her own, or not, was heartbreaking. She was part of the family.

My life as I know it began in 1973 at the French Hospital in Manhattan, entering a world that seemed perfectly aligned. My father had already secured a slice of the American Dream for us: a proper house, a big yard, and a family that included my big sister Nancy and our older brother Hans, from dad's previous relationship. In those early years, I was the classic "Daddy's little girl," the final piece of the stable life he was building.

Back then, home was a single-family house on a quiet suburban block in Laurelton, Queens. My parents, Fritz and Ginette, arrived from Haiti in the early 1960s, two people among a wave of immigrants chasing the American dream. Even though they both grew up in Port-au-Prince, their roots reached back to different corners of the island. My mom's dad was from Tiburon, and my dad's family was from Saint Marc.

I still see my mother in our kitchen, dancing with a wooden spoon to show us how they met. She loved telling that story. Despite her small, five-foot frame, she seemed to grow as she recreated that night at a party in Brooklyn. She would mimic her younger self, swirling in a tiny polka-dot mini dress with her hair in a perfect bouffant. In her mind, she was still that girl who danced the night away and won over the man who would build her a life.

Mom was a homemaker who cooked, cleaned, and cared for us while Dad was at work. Dad was a manager at a couple of parking garages in Manhattan. He was highly entrepreneurial, owning two yellow taxicabs and an apartment complex in Brooklyn. I loved the joy of watching him pull into the driveway at home in his oversized car. Dad spoiled Mom and bought her a black Mercedes-Benz, though I don't have any memories of it. We were a typical, comfortable middle-class family.

As one of the first of seven sisters to come over from Haiti, my mom opened our home to the rest of the family, and our house became a landing pad for aunts and cousins fresh off the plane. My parents had built a real haven, a refuge. The basement served as our lively hub, anchoring every big family party we threw. Mom would cook up a storm, and the house was always packed and festive.

Several neighbors were also Haitian immigrants, friends whom my dad convinced to buy houses near us. As children, we would all play up and down the block, riding bicycles, jumping rope, playing hopscotch, all the while keeping an eye out for any danger signs. The biggest risk was someone's dog getting loose and chasing us down. There were so many times I remember running so fast to save my own life, and often jumping up and climbing on top of someone's parked car to find safety. Those were great, fun times!

That life feels like something from a storybook compared to what came next.

In 1977, when I was four, my parents divorced, and everything changed. That word, divorced, sounds too clean, too administrative, for what actually happened. Because my father didn't just leave, he disappeared. No weekends. No visits. No child support. No explanations. Just gone.

Some people place blame on others, who supposedly did "things" to keep him away from us, and that the situation was complicated. But I don't buy that. He was an adult. If he really cared, he would have made up his own mind and fought for us. Supposedly, I was his precious little girl.

My mother, once a full-time homemaker, had to pivot. She picked up the pieces while he went on with his life, including remarrying and having other children. The immediate fallout was clear: we had to move. Suddenly, everything I knew to be true vanished. It was the start of an unstable rhythm as we drifted from house to house across Queens and Long Island, punctuated by short stints boarding with family. For a long time, "home" was not a place, but a series of temporary stops.

First, we moved across the street to live with Mom's friend, another Haitian family. Next, a townhouse on a quiet, tree-lined street became our home in Hollis. We rented one side of a two-family house, and for a while, a new sense of normalcy took hold. The landlord was a friend of my mom's from Haiti.

The next moves are a bit of a blur. One place I clearly remember is the basement apartment on Guy R. Brewer Boulevard in Jamaica, Queens. It was small, dark, and sat right on a busy corner. It had two bedrooms, Mom in one, Nancy and I crammed into the other. The ceilings felt low, and the rooms were packed tight. Unfortunately, we weren't the only tenants that claimed occupancy there. Much to our horror, mice would frequently pay us unannounced visits and sprint across the room, completely freaking us out! Nancy and I would jump up on the furniture, including tabletops, and scream, while our mom would get a broom and try to shoo them away.

Then came 218th Street and Merrick Boulevard, back in Laurelton, the last place I would call home before leaving for college. It was a second-floor apartment in a split house, two bedrooms, a kitchen, one bath, and a living room that served as the true hub of the house. Nancy and I shared a bedroom as usual with two twin beds, matching nightstands, one dresser, and a small closet. I plastered my side of the room with cutouts and posters of my favorite musicians and celebrities from iconic magazines like Right On! and Word Up! Most notably, I had a special section just for my biggest crush, LL Cool J, including a life-sized poster of him on the closet door.

My mother loved to cook, and her food was delicious, but given the various jobs she was juggling, she didn't always have time to prepare a home-cooked meal for us. Struggling to keep everything afloat, she received state public assistance, including food stamps. I can still vividly see the government-issued big rectangular block of cheddar cheese in our refrigerator and how I used to make sandwiches with it on white Wonder Bread. Moving from place to place also meant I moved schools a lot.

I spent my early years at Saint Clare Catholic Academy in Rosedale, back when my parents were still together. They even hired a driver to take my sister and me to and from school. Growing up in a Haitian family meant you were raised Catholic and expected to act like it. Catholic school meant discipline, and the nuns did not hesitate to give you a taste of their rulers, as I would come to experience, unfortunately, from time to time.

By fifth grade, I was at Saint Joachim and Anne, another Catholic school in Queens Village. We were still in the middle of a post-divorce transition, living with one of my aunts. That was just for a year or so, and then we moved again. By the time we landed in Hollis next, the money had changed. We couldn't afford private school anymore, so I switched to a public school for the first time.

Middle school was at Linden Junior High School, also known as Intermediate School (IS) 192. I landed a spot in the Special Progress (SP) class, the gifted program, which felt like a badge back then. I was there for sixth grade, seventh grade, and then - get this - I skipped eighth and jumped straight to ninth grade. Who does that?! I had no idea that it was part of the program, so I felt pretty special and smart. It was the first time I began learning a language not spoken at home. I took on Spanish and really got good at it back then. I was also inducted into the National Honor Society, but didn't think much of it at the time. My classmates and I were definitely considered the geeks of our school, but I didn't care. We were ahead of the pack, and I enjoyed the academic rigor.

After IS 192, I attended Hillcrest High School in Jamaica, Queens, as part of the class of '90. Our high school was situated off Hillside Avenue and offered tracks unlike most other schools. I chose the Theater Arts academy while others chose Medical Assistant, Nursing, Finance, etc. Hillcrest High is where I spent my tenth, eleventh, and twelfth grades, and where many good memories live. I spent most of my days in the school theater, on the stage, and in between classes like Advanced Placement English.

Getting to Hillcrest each day meant learning the city on my own, one routine at a time. I rode the Q5 bus to the Jamaica Avenue terminal, a familiar route that carried me from neighborhood quiet into the steady pulse of Jamaica. Across the street stood the Queens

Public Library, a place I returned to often after school to read, to think, or simply to sit in calm before heading home. Just beyond it, the Colosseum Mall buzzed with life. Music drifted from sneaker shops, window displays flashed oversized denim and bold gold chains, and places like Shirt Kings felt less like stores than cultural landmarks. I rarely bought anything. Mostly, I lingered, watching people, absorbing style, sound, and confidence. Somewhere between that bus ride, those storefronts, and the walk back home, I was learning independence. I was figuring out how to move through the world alone, alert, and curious, long before I ever stepped onto a stage.

All that independence and confidence I'd been gathering on the Q5 and on Jamaica Ave finally paid off. I can safely say my senior year was the best. We were responsible for creating our own full-scale final-year production, "The Best Years of Our Lives," where we all had a chance to write parts of the screenplay, sing and act in various roles, help build the props, and control the lighting. Before graduation, we were inducted into the International Thespian Society as lifetime members. I was an actress, and I loved it.

In addition to excelling academically, I was active in school politics. Our principal nominated me as one of Queens' "Super Youth." I was so proud to see my name appear in a multi-page Daily News article titled "A Salute to New York's Best and Brightest."

I also found my voice and enough courage to get involved with public activism for the first time. I took part in a big protest surrounding the arrest of a student named Justice on school grounds.

I don't remember what the police were charging him with, but we took issue with it happening inside the school, which was supposed to be a haven for us. I was out on the front lines of the rally with friends like Nyesha, who could stare down anyone boldly, and Jasmine, who didn't even need a megaphone because her voice reverberated across town.

We walked out of class and stood on the school's front plaza, chanting "No Justice, No Peace" with poster boards and bullhorns.

There was media coverage, and the school administration issued an apology and promised to look further into the matter. That was the first time I experienced the power of collective voice and action firsthand, and it felt good.

When the Daily News called me one of the 'Best and Brightest,' they saw my grades, but they didn't see the basement or the food stamps. I realized then that my voice was a tool. Whether I was on a theatrical stage or demanding justice, I was learning that resilience isn't just about 'getting through.' It's about working hard and showing up with such excellence that the world has no choice but to acknowledge you, regardless of where you come from.

Watching my mother move through the world defined my own work ethic; she was the blueprint for how I showed up every day. After the divorce, she worked very hard and hustled to provide for us. In addition to the various jobs she was juggling, she also cared for and babysat other people's kids. She even went so far as to pawn her gold jewelry and precious stones to get cash loans, anything to keep rent paid and food on the table. To her credit, we were never hungry and always had a roof over our heads. She paid the bills and kept the fridge stocked, making sure we had what we needed.

It wasn't until recently, after my mom passed away, while Nancy and I were sifting through her old papers, that I began to grasp the full scope of my mom's effort. Among her things, we found her divorce certificate and a résumé that told a story I never fully knew.

Looking at those pages now, through the eyes of a professional who has spent decades analyzing human capacity, I don't just see a list of jobs. I see a master class in the art of pivot. My mother went from being an unemployed housewife to a vocational student, then to a hospital accounting assistant, and eventually a certified nursing assistant. She didn't have the luxury of "finding her passion" or waiting for the perfect conditions. She simply looked at the dissolution of her marriage, saw two hungry children, and decided that excellence and grit were our only way out.

Her life taught me that your starting point is not your finish line. Mom was the original diplomat; she negotiated with landlords, navigated the labyrinth of state public assistance, and managed the limited resources of a "government cheese" budget with the precision of a chief financial officer. She proved that you don't need an oversized mahogany desk to lead. You just need the resolve to keep moving, and the faith that something greater is steadying your steps.

Every time my mom moved us to a new apartment, she was silently teaching me that the human spirit is portable. You don't leave your dignity behind just because you're leaving a house. You pack it up, you pivot, and you build again. I realize now that I didn't become a leader within the US Government just like that. I was born into a leadership academy run by a woman who refused to let the place where my father left us become our permanent address.

As I've grown older, I've realized that I didn't just inherit my mother's eyes or her love for a good meal; I inherited her bones. I call them my resilient, imperfect bones. They aren't the smooth, polished bones of someone who has lived a life of ease and predictable weather. Instead, they are the hardened, structural bones of a woman who had to resist and stand tall when the foundation of her life was crumbling.

My mother's resilience was the skeletal architecture of our survival. I am beginning to fully grasp the depth of that strength now. My ability to walk into a room in Washington or a village in the Pacific and hold my ground comes from being lifted by the very bones she passed on to me.

As for my dad, I stopped waiting for him to come back. But I never stopped noticing he was gone.

Sometimes I think he thought he was doing us a favor, leaving us with our mother, staying far enough away that we couldn't find our way back to him. I didn't ask questions. I just stayed focused. I wanted to be good, good in school, good at surviving. Whatever that meant. I didn't have time to fall apart.

As we got older, Nancy and I reconnected with our brother, Hans. After our parents' divorce, he moved around to a few places, but eventually married in 1985 and moved his family to Florida. We started visiting them there, and he'd give us updates on our dad and our younger brothers.

After a while, our dad also relocated to Florida with his new family.

At some point, I decided to try to bridge the distance with my dad. I took the initiative to visit him from time to time, holding onto the hope that the mystery of his disappearance could be solved. I'd ask myself: did he ever really care?

Well, yes. Every time I go to see him, my doubts are silenced by the way his eyes light up when I walk into the room, and he jokingly calls me "fatso," like he used to when I was younger. I've never been a skinny person, and I get my big bones from him. He's a big and tall guy, so I'm just a shorter version of him. I usually just roll my eyes, giggle nervously, and sit back ready to soak up any information he cares to share.

I remember this one time, Anthony and I went to visit him, and he told us a story, the milk story. He said that when I was about one year old, he came home from a long day at work, tired. I ran to greet him in the driveway and said, "Daddy, the milk is finished." So, without hesitation, he turned around and went right back out to buy some. When he returned, it was pouring rain, and he came into the house soaking wet. I looked up at him and said, "Poor Daddy." And he just laughed as he put the milk in the refrigerator.

That story still deepens the mystery for me. If he cared so much then, what changed?

As I write this, my father is over 90 years old, has had a few strokes, and can no longer walk unassisted. And yet, the feeling persists: he's still the man who dumped Princess and never looked back. The man who deserted us, too.

He drove Princess far away so she couldn't find her way back. For him, perhaps, distance alone could heal the broken pieces of our family. Maybe he thought out of sight meant out of pain.

I've spent a good part of my adult years trying to prove that wasn't true, trying to build a relationship with him, to forgive and forget and move on because that's what I do. And because life is easier that way, for me at least.

Not long ago, I decided to throw him a surprise milestone birthday party. His 90th. Coordinating with all my siblings, we invited people, rented a venue, hired a caterer, and got the cake and decorations. Family members came in from out of town. The plan was for his wife to bring him. We waited for hours. We called and tried to convince him to come. He claimed he wasn't feeling well and didn't show up.

And in that moment, standing in a rented hall with a cake that he would never cut, I realized that my father's disappearance wasn't my failure. It was his loss. Maybe he left us behind, hoping we wouldn't find our way back, but he underestimated the Haitian blood in my veins and the Queens grit in my bones. I didn't find my way back to the life he abandoned; I built a better one on the way. Excellence was my north star, and resilience became my compass.

Sitting in our Laurelton living room with my mom and Nancy. This was the backdrop of my early years in Queens, long before life got complicated. I look at this now and see the version of us that existed before the divorce redefined what home meant.

Chapter Two

THE FAMILY WE HIDE

To be the child of immigrants is to be automatically born with a dual passport, one for the world everyone sees and one for the world only your blood understands.

I walked into the hallways of I.S. 192, thinking I'd finally found my place. The school buzzed with a rhythm I knew by heart, the loud laughter echoing off lockers, the quick shuffle of sneakers, and that distinct mix of Hollis, Queens' attitude. After years in stiff Catholic-school uniforms and hushed classrooms, this felt like breathing room. Walking into a school filled almost entirely with Black Americans, I thought I finally belonged.

Then, the new kids arrived.

An influx of immigrant children who were not born in the U.S. arrived, and the school formed a special class for them in a separate part of the building. They were Black, but different. They didn't speak English, so they were enrolled in the English as a Second Language program. I didn't know where they were from until I started hearing my peers call them derogatory names.

"Haitian booty scratcher."

"Fresh off the boat."

They laughed about how those kids smelled like poverty. The jokes spread like a stain, and I listened in silence, knowing precisely who they were talking about. These kids were from Haiti. They shared the same blood as my mom and the aunts and cousins who'd crowded our basement with laughter and the smell of *griot*. But I didn't say a word.

Sometimes I wonder: who teaches a twelve-year-old to hate what they see in the mirror? Who teaches us to dislike the essence of what makes us? I didn't have an answer then. I only had fear, the old terror of being pushed back to the outside. So, I did something that still weighs on me: I distanced myself. I watched them from across the cafeteria, as if they were strangers. I buried my Creole phrases deep and sharpened my English, making sure no one could ever lump me in with the "others."

This was also a time when Haiti carried a stigma far heavier than poverty. It had been publicly marked as a source of HIV and AIDS, and that label gave cruelty permission to thrive. Too young and too unsure of myself, I learned quickly that survival sometimes meant silence and hiding parts of who I was.

I wasn't mature enough yet to see that by turning away from them, I was turning away from the very architecture of my soul, the part of me that would one day bridge worlds. I'm not proud of it. I sometimes wonder where those kids are now and whether they ever realized that the girl in the gifted classes was secretly their sister, too scared to say hello.

On reflection, I may have had my reasons for hiding. It's challenging to act as a support for others when your own footing is shaky. My mother lived in her own world, ruled by routines and shadows that didn't align with the 'Best and Brightest' image I aspired to at school.

The drinking, which I had seen turn joyful gatherings into embarrassments, was just the start. My mother drank for as long as I could remember, long before I understood what alcoholism was or had language for how it reordered a family's center of gravity. At celebrations meant to bring us together, her drinking often pulled her away instead. Nancy and I were left to manage the quiet embarrassment, the whispered apologies, and, at times, the physical task of helping her get home safely.

Then there were the Salem cigarettes, constant and ever-present in their green and white packets. She was a heavy chain-smoker, and Nancy and I were often her couriers, sent to the corner store or gas station to buy pack after pack. In time, gambling joined the mix, bringing a different kind of reckoning altogether.

On weekends when it was my mom's turn to host poker night, the kitchen table would disappear under a green felt cloth. The air would grow thick with cigarette smoke and the sharp, medicinal smell of Barbancourt rum. I'd watch my mother, her face unreadable and her fingers yellowed from nicotine, holding court at the table for hours with three or four men, absorbed and resolute. She would sip, deal, and sip again. I'd go to bed worrying: Would she be awake in the morning? How much money was slipping through her fingers? Often, we'd wake up only to find them still playing, the house smelling of stale smoke and bloodshot eyes staring back at us as we darted by.

When she wasn't at the poker table, she was chasing the lottery, buying tickets in stacks or running numbers with local Haitian bookies playing Borlette. She was hunting for a better life, or maybe just the rush of almost winning. That hunt made our home life feel unpredictable.

Sometimes our world was just strange and funny, like the year no one wanted to take down the Christmas tree. My mother simply threw a white sheet over it and let it stand until April, a ghostly fixture in our living room that we all learned to walk around and ignore. Other times, the world felt erratic. I can still see her chasing me around the apartment with a broom like a madwoman because I'd come home past a deadline she'd suddenly decided mattered.

Yet, amid all that chaos, there were still flashes of the mother I loved the most. We would sit together watching Wheel of Fortune and Jeopardy!, shouting out answers at the TV. Other times, she was our resident hairstylist, washing and setting our hair in big rollers. Though we endured hours of torture under the hair dryer, the final reveal of our bouncy, luxurious curls made every minute worth it.

Music filled those moments, too. She loved to sing along to her favorite songs by Mireille Mathieu or Tabou Combo, and we would join in, our voices rising together as if nothing else in the world mattered. Those are the kinds of moments I return to. I often wished those moments could stretch on longer.

Still, as my mother navigated largely unseen challenges, the steadiness I needed often came from my older sister, Nancy. Nancy has always been a natural caretaker, the kind of person who looks after everyone, even those who don't know how to say thank you. I am forever grateful for how she stepped into the gap. She made sure my outfits were on point, and I left for school on time. As I got older, she did more than just care for me; she pulled me under her wing and into her world.

She became my gateway to the one place where I started to truly feel alive, the streets and the sounds of New York. I'd hang out with Nancy and her friends, sneak into parties and clubs, and sometimes even take the train to Manhattan to dance until our legs gave out. Her friends became my friends.

Our friends became part of my stability, including La'Zette and Sheldra, my girls from middle school; the twins, Tina and Trina; the sisters, Shirley, and Milly; Rhonda and Toni; and some of our cousins. For some reason that I can't remember now, Shirley started calling us by a nickname, "cambo," short for Cambodians, and that stuck. Mind you, none of us had been to Cambodia at that time, but until this day, we all call each other *cambos* as a term of endearment.

When we went out, we gave ourselves names that felt like beauty and power: I was Ebony, La'Zette was Essence, and Shel was Mahogany. You couldn't tell us anything. We were "cool geeks" who chose clean fun over trouble, losing ourselves in the rhythm of the city that never sleeps.

Queens in those days was alive with music. You could walk a few blocks and hear three different rhythms drifting from windows or backyards. Someone would say, "Something is happening over on 225th," and off we'd go, following the sound on foot. It was pure enjoyment, just music and dancing, cute outfits and jewelry (including our Salt N Pepa-inspired catsuits), and the sweet taste of being young and invincible.

Our crew wasn't troublemakers, but we did have a healthy enough dose of risk-taking that expanded our horizons beyond Queens' borders. We thought nothing of hopping into the informal "dollar vans," at all hours of the night, driven by Caribbean men, with bass-heavy soca and reggae blasting like a moving block party. We'd pile in, lip gloss on, and outfits tight, zigzagging down Merrick Boulevard toward the E or F train, the gateway to our city nights. Those hour-long treks were the warm-up for legendary spots like The Tunnel, The Underground, Studio 54, and Bentley's.

My passion for hip hop was so intense that when Trina managed to get the famous Erick Sermon's phone number for me after an EPMD concert, I actually called him. To my surprise, he drove his signature Mercedes-Benz all the way from Long Island to my apartment in Laurelton. I was in awe of his larger-than-life presence. He was so tall that he had to bend to walk through our doorway, yet he sat in our living room, chatting with me and Shel like old friends. It was a surreal moment, filled with pure and unexpected magic.

Nancy and I grew up without fences, curfews, check-ins, or hovering. By some miracle, we stayed on track. We seemed to know instinctively where the edge was, and we didn't step off it. Perhaps it was a miracle, but it was also a conscious choice, shaped by watching the person we loved most struggle to keep her own life together.

I still don't know, even to this day, how many of our friends, if any, truly understood what was happening at home or what my sister and I were quietly carrying when it came to our mom and her dependencies. If anyone did know, they never made us feel different, never brought awkwardness or pity into our space. It was only acceptance, laughter, and the comfort of being treated just like everyone else. It's just as possible they had no idea, and honestly, that ignorance was a blessing. Not having to explain, justify, or shrink ourselves around the weight of our reality gave us room to breathe. It allowed us moments of escape and time to simply be young, happy-go-lucky, and feel normal.

But even in those carefree moments, I was carrying a secret far heavier than our "normal" life suggested, a part of my heritage I have kept tucked away until now.

While my friends saw the "Best and Brightest" girl, they didn't see the side of our culture that the world often fears and misunderstands. I grew up navigating an unspoken tension between two worlds: the fun-loving, studious girl and the daughter of a family that practiced ancient traditions some would consider taboo.

For a long time, this was my deepest fear. I was terrified that if people knew, they would see me as "other" in a way I could never come back from. So, I wore my mask, never breathing a word about the ceremonies or the otherworldly energy that would sometimes fill our living room.

What made these practices most daunting was that they were never just about spirituality or connecting with another world. There was often a darker undercurrent, a cycle of vendettas, spell-casting, and a constant back-and-forth of "protection" and "attacks."

My mom and some of her sisters had a long history of love-hate relationships. One day, they would be inseparable; the next, they wouldn't speak for years. This same volatility bled into their friend circles, and my mother constantly warned me about having too many friends or being too trusting.

For Haitians, and I'm sure in some other cultures too, this kind of toxicity is where things could get dangerous. A feud didn't just mean giving someone the silent treatment or cutting them off. It had the potential to carry something deeper: casting spells on each other. Yes, I'm talking about Voodoo here. The kind that you've seen and read about in movies and books about Haiti. My mother and some family members actively practiced Voodoo while simultaneously being Roman Catholics. You hear about these "crazy" things happening, but you never expect them to land on your own doorstep or strike your own loved ones.

Then there was the time when the danger hit close to home. Someone targeted one of our family members with a spell, but because she was spiritually shielded, the harm passed her by. Instead, the curse hunted for a weaker link, sliding down to the next person in line. Unfortunately, that person was one of my cousins.

I didn't believe it. Not then. It was shocking and scary.

I must have been in the later years of elementary school when this happened, so I asked one of my older cousins who was there to tell me what happened. According to him, the nightmare began in the middle of the night while everyone was sleeping. One of our cousins began to move strangely, and at first, the others thought it was just a bad dream. Then a sound filled the room, as if a giant bird had gotten inside and was making loud, squawking noises. The body jerked once, then twice, as though it no longer belonged to our relative. Their eyes rolled back into their head as they jumped up, stomping and thrashing back and forth across the apartment.

My older cousin, a tall, broad-shouldered man who could carry a sofa up a flight of stairs without breaking a sweat, told me what happened next. He had lunged forward to hold them down, but our possessed cousin broke free from his grip as if he were a child. The energy in the room shifted instantly. People were gasping and shouting in Creole while someone scrambled for water. Downstairs, the neighbors were already on the phone, calling 911.

It took several grown men to hold them, but the body kept twisting and kicking. The voice coming out of them was a piercing, strange growl that sounded nothing like the person we knew. By the time the police arrived, the living room was a scene of chaos. Family members had shoved furniture aside, and my mom, aunts and cousins huddled in a circle of panic and prayer. No one quite remembers how they were finally subdued, only that an ambulance eventually arrived and took them away into the night.

The aftermath was long and grueling. My cousin stayed in the hospital for seven months in a coma, fading into someone unrecognizable. They lay still in the hospital bed, their tongue swollen and hanging past their lips all the way down to their chest. I remember feeling physically sick when I saw that image in my mind, asking myself what in the world was happening to my family.

The doctors ran every test available, but nothing made sense. There was no clear diagnosis, just a mystery that medical professionals and Western medicine were powerless to solve. Without any other explanation, they eventually labeled it a psychotic episode. However, one of the doctors, a Haitian man who understood the cultural undercurrents, suggested to my aunt that she take them back to Haiti to see a spiritual healer called a Mambo. My aunt didn't need to be convinced; she already knew the answer lay there.

A few days after my cousin's discharge, we packed our suitcases. My aunt asked my mother for her help, calling on her spiritual strength for the journey ahead. Because she couldn't leave Nancy and me behind, my mother swept us into the mission. It was my first time visiting the island. At twelve or thirteen, I forced myself to feel excited, trying to drown out the recent chaos with visions of palm trees, white sand, and the cousins I had never met.

The reality was far different. Soon after landing in Port au Prince, we bypassed the tropical scenery and drove far from the city, deep into a countryside that looked more like a scene from a mystery movie. The silence of the rural landscape was broken only by the sound of a goat tied just inside a tall, rusting gate. Its small hooves kicked at the dirt, a desperate and lonely sound. The moment I saw it, a chill ran through me. I knew, even without anyone saying it out loud, that the goat represented the thin line between life and death.

The air inside the compound was thick and tasted of old smoke and the sharp, copper tang of something metallic. I felt a wave of nausea hit me, and for a second, I thought I might actually get sick right there in the dirt. I fought the urge to pinch my nose, knowing it would embarrass my mother in front of the Mambo, so I just took shallow, careful breaths instead. Nancy and I huddled close together, our shoulders touching. We didn't say anything, but we were constantly exchanging wide-eyed looks. It was our silent language, a way of asking, *are you seeing this? Is this actually happening?*

My mother must have sensed our discomfort because she shot us a sharp, warning look that told us to get ourselves together. She, along with my aunt and the Mambo, led us toward a cemetery that felt like another world entirely. It was nothing like the orderly, manicured graveyards of New York. Instead, we entered a crowded city for the dead, where miniature houses served as graves, their small doors sporting coats of faded blue and red paint.

My mom whispered to us, "We have to knock."

"Knock?" I asked, my voice barely audible.

We had to knock to wake the spirits up so they would know we were there. I looked at Nancy, my eyes pleading with her to go first, and I nudged her with my elbow as if to say, *you do it.* She nudged me right back, her face pulled into a "no way" expression, and for a split second, we were just two sisters arguing over a chore. But my mother's gaze was on us again, and I knew I didn't have a choice.

I watched as my mother rapped her knuckles on the cement, her movements slow and deliberate, before stepping aside to make room for me. My hand hesitated as I felt the cool, damp surface of the tomb. I finally forced myself to tap once, then twice.

My mind was racing, picturing what could be waiting on the other side. I imagined a skeleton, or something ancient, covered in cobwebs and dirt. I wondered whether the spirits had eyes or would simply float out through the stone. I tried to tell myself it was just tradition, just culture, but my skin crawled in protest. Every instinct I had was screaming at me to run, not to wake the dead.

The ritual stretched on for half an hour. When the Mambo finally signaled the end, we returned to the compound where a small crowd had gathered in one of the rooms. They began to sing and chant, low at first, then louder, until the rhythm built as if the earth itself was joining in. Unfamiliar symbols, drawn in white chalk, were carved into the dirt floor. Pictures and statues of various saints, lined up with burning candles, surrounded us.

Then, the Mambo slit the throat of a chicken. I watched, transfixed by a dreadful act I had only ever seen in movies like *The Serpent and the Rainbow*. Its wings beat furiously against the Mambo's arm in a final, desperate struggle until they stilled. Nearby, a man crouched low, steadying a hollow gourd to collect every drop of the chicken's blood as it fell. Next, they dug a shallow pit in the dirt floor, just wide enough for my cousin to lie in. My lungs suddenly refused to work. This execution did not look like a ritual; it looked like a burial. I wondered if this was the end and if this was truly why we had come all this way.

My cousin climbed in without protest, eyes fixed on the ceiling. Someone sprinkled Florida Water over them while others waved burning herbs and traced patterns in the air. The chicken's blood was dabbed onto their skin, making the sign of the cross. I stood at the edge, frozen. Part of me wanted to pull them out, but the other part knew that in this place, I had no power. At the time, I was just a terrified girl watching a grave dug in a dirt floor. I did not yet understand the symbolism that they were performing a mock burial to exorcise the evil spirit and leave it behind in the earth.

Hours later, once the ceremony concluded, the crowd broke into a triumphant celebration, piercing spirit-calls and rhythmic dancing. The danger had passed. My aunt and mother looked relieved. My cousin was quiet but walking on their own.

I thought the ritual had finally released us, but the Mambo stopped us with a final, chilling instruction.

"If you find the goat at the gate and it is no longer alive," she said, "then everything worked according to the plan."

We stepped back out through the gate and saw the goat lying in the dust, quiet and stiff, its eyes clouded. I quickly looked away, terrified.

I said nothing. I did not ask about the knocking, the blood, the songs, or the goat. I did not talk about it when we got back to New York, either. No one did. The memory was too strange, and I knew how Americans spoke about Voodoo. I did not want that look or to be associated with it. I tucked the entire experience away, vowing never to talk about it. Like all our other secrets, it became a heavyweight sealed tight inside me.

Some secrets, however, are just hard to hide. You would think a ceremony like the one in Haiti was a rare, one-time event, but these rituals became a somewhat ordinary part of my world. With the constant bad blood between rivals and the belief that you had to keep the ancestors pleased to maintain your protection, it seemed my mother was always performing rituals or providing offerings to stay on top. I have nothing against those who practice. In fact, as I have traveled the world, I have come to appreciate that many different cultures have their own unique spiritual practices. Some are similar to what I saw in Haiti, such as the traditions of the *Sangomas* in South Africa. But for me, the cost was too high. The Haitian spiritual path seemed like a life of constant maintenance, fueled by the fear of what awaited us if we ever looked away. I did not want to inherit that responsibility, and I especially did not want to inherit the darkness. Even as a child, I knew this was not the life I wanted. Somewhere in the middle of it all, I started quietly preparing to leave.

I learned independence early, though not in the typical teenage ways of rebellion and rule-bending. By 15, I was already working, first as a cashier at Roy Rogers and later at a Carlton Cards store in Green Acres Mall in Valley Stream, Long Island. Earning my own paycheck taught me that independence wasn't just about freedom. It was about responsibility and learning to carry myself while carrying my books.

Balancing work on weekends with my studies during the week was tough, but it was about more than just a paycheck. Receiving my first one was a pivotal moment. Holding that check felt like evidence I had the power to change my circumstances. While the discounts and free meals were nice perks, they were just the icing on the cake. My motivation extended far beyond financial gain. I was more interested in building a better life for myself.

Looking back, I wonder though. Could this be where my actual training began? Long before I ever set foot in a foreign embassy or sat across from a head of state, I was already a dual citizen of two incompatible worlds. The very secrets I tried to hide were shaping me. The structural resilience I inherited from my mother came with a steep price: bones that were strong but weary from the weight of what stayed unsaid. I spent years trying to get away, thinking that if I ran far enough, to Manhattan, to college, to the ends of the earth, I could leave the spirits behind. I wanted a light life. I wanted a future not dictated by the contents of a hollow gourd or by the sacrifice of a goat.

But as I began to pack my bags, preparing to leave for the next chapter of my life, I realized that you do not just leave your history behind. You carry it in your marrow. I was heading toward a world of resumes and prestigious titles, but the echoes of those Haitian drums were coming with me. I was ready to leave the shadows, but the shadows, I would soon find out, were not quite finished with me.

Hanging out with some of my cousins and friends in Laurelton.

Chapter Three

BEYOND THE BOROUGHS

As I approached my senior year at Hillcrest, I began thinking about college. I wanted to go to Harvard University. "Harvard?"

My guidance counselor didn't argue. She laughed, a small breath through her nose.

"Let's be realistic," she said. "Aim for something attainable."

I took that rejection home with me, still clinging to my true dream: performing on stage. Acting was like breath to me. However, my mother quickly closed that door. To her, acting wouldn't pay the bills; she saw it as a silly dream and a quick route to a life of hardship.

"Medicine. Law. Engineering," she commanded, naming the three pillars of Haitian survival. "In this country, you don't make-believe. You build. You work. Real work."

My counselor had already decided how far I could go. My mother had already decided who I was allowed to be. So I let Harvard go. I let Broadway and Hollywood go. I pulled out some brochures and chose a compromise: Syracuse.

The compromise, however, came at a steep price. Tuition was astronomical, and since my mother couldn't afford it, I had to shoulder the burden myself. I signed for student loans that would sit like a weight on my back for years to come, but I signed anyway. I was determined to get an education on my own terms, no matter the cost.

I knew I'd have to take on-campus jobs and chase down every shift I could find to stay afloat. Every dollar I'd earn would be a step toward my own sovereignty. Choosing Syracuse was a gamble, but a practical one because it was still in New York. It was close to home, but not too close. Just far enough away to escape and be on my own.

I wasn't going to Cambridge. I wasn't going to the stage.

I was at least going somewhere I could finally be on my own terms.

At only sixteen, I graduated high school and moved upstate to Syracuse. I joined the university's Summer Institute, a pre-orientation program for underrepresented students to ease our transition into college. Syracuse is a Predominantly White Institution that only had 7% or so of students of color on campus at that time. Starting two months before the first semester gave us an early start and helped build a sense of community.

When the fall semester began, I moved into a dorm on campus. My first college roommate, a kind, welcoming Italian-American young lady named Tracie, was assigned to share the room with me. We hit it off immediately. Tracie's warmth and friendliness made the transition smoother, and we quickly became close friends. Our bond grew stronger over the years, and even though we went our separate ways when I studied abroad, we remained close. To this day, we are still in touch. She was among the first to help make that new universe feel like home, and I love her like a sister.

One of the most memorable experiences was the sense of camaraderie I felt with other students of color. I became actively involved with student organizations on campus, including those that led the South African anti-apartheid movement. I also served as

President of the Black Artists League, which celebrated student artists of color through a magazine we published and events we curated throughout the school year.

I organized campus events featuring major acts like Digable Planets. I also co-edited the League's flagship magazine, Kuumba, which showcased the work of talented student artists such as Shane Evans and Darrin Deas. Through these activities, I discovered a sense of belonging I hadn't experienced before. I was no longer just a student; I became part of a community that understood and supported me.

I also met other good friends, such as Veronica, a Dominican powerhouse, through classes in the African American Studies department, who remain close to this day. There were others, like Alison, who was also from Laurelton, with whom I went to the same high school in Queens. It was this network of support and friendship that carried me through my college years. I remember the parties at the Underground or on South Campus, the laughter, and the late-night conversations. We would gather in the dining hall or library, sharing stories and tips, creating a space where we could be ourselves.

One thing about me, though, is that I was a stickler for rules. Disciplined.

While some of my friends spent their weekends drinking cheap beer and getting lost in the heavy haze of weed at the parties, I was the girl with focused, clear eyes and a steady, sober hold on my drink. I barely touched alcohol until I was twenty-one, not because I didn't know how to have fun. I was just comfortable with clean fun, and I still had a good time.

Besides, my real "party" was happening somewhere else. It lived in the library's quiet aisles and slowly made its way into the deeper corners of my soul. It was at Syracuse that I began to explore my Haitian heritage with intention.

For the first time, I began to peel back the layers of Haiti and what it meant to be Haitian. I stopped seeing Haiti through the lens of fear and started seeing it through the lens of power. I discovered a history that wasn't about "superstition" but about revolution and sovereignty.

I read about Toussaint Louverture and Jean-Jacques Dessalines, men who didn't just ask for freedom but seized it, orchestrating the only successful slave revolt in human history. I traced my own bloodline back across the Atlantic, realizing that my African roots had made a legendary pit stop in the Caribbean before ever reaching New York. Haiti wasn't just a place on a map where people knocked on graves and buried goats. It was the world's first independent Black republic. It was a lighthouse and a model of resistance for the rest of the world.

The more I learned, the more I realized how remarkable Haiti was and how proud I should be of my roots. The bones I carried weren't a curse; they were a heritage of triumph. I wasn't just a girl from Queens trying to fit in. I was a descendant of revolutionaries. I belonged to a people who, even in the face of overwhelming adversity, could rise and claim their freedom. That awakening took on a Pan-African lens.

While taking my International Relations courses, I developed a keen interest in Africa, particularly the Black experience across the diaspora. I took classes in the African American Studies department with brilliant and revolutionary professors such as Horace Campbell from Jamaica, Micere Mugo from Kenya, S.N. Sangapam from the Democratic Republic of Congo, and Janis Mayes from the U.S. I delved into the works of writers such as Nawal El Saadawi, Frantz Fanon, Marcus Garvey, C.L.R. James, and Walter Rodney.

In my final year, I joined a group of students to advocate to the school administration for the creation of a study abroad program in Africa.

In the fall of 1993, I, along with about a dozen other pioneering students, left for a semester in Zimbabwe, led by Professor Campbell. That was my first time visiting the Motherland, and it helped cement my love not only for the continent but also for international travel and cultural exchange.

Harare was nothing like the "frozen-in-time" Africa I had seen on television. I found a city with wide, paved roads lined with jacaranda trees that showered the sidewalks with purple blossoms. Victorian architecture stood shoulder to shoulder with modern high-rises. In the mornings, the streets belonged to men in sharp suits and children in crisp uniforms. The city moved with an organized, fast-paced, and entirely normal rhythm.

I lived in Mabelreign, an upscale suburb where large homes sat behind tall walls and heavy gates. My host family treated me like their own; hospitality wasn't a gesture there, it was a way of life. Every morning, the smell of maize porridge and the tea kettle whistle from the kitchen signaled the start of a new lesson.

At the SAPES Trust, professors from the University of Zimbabwe brought history and economics to life in small, intimate classrooms. These weren't dull academic exercises. They were intense, lively battlegrounds where we dissected liberation movements of the frontline states and Africa's place in the global order. I traded insights with local students who weren't just studying history. They were the children of it.

We balanced the weight of those debates with the rhythm of the city. We discovered places like Nandos that had the best grilled chicken in town. We became regulars at clubs like Turtles and Circus, where DJs spun hip hop, reggae, and R&B. Even there, as the youngest of the group who stayed sober as the room blurred, I was learning. I watched in awe as a supposedly foreign culture celebrated itself, realizing how similar it was to my own.

We traveled to the ruins of Great Zimbabwe and the mist of Victoria Falls, but it was the overland trips across the borders that truly sharpened my lens.

En route to Lusaka, Zambia, the beauty was expansive and captivating as I went on safari for the first time and came face to face with fierce hippos in the Zambezi. But in Mozambique, I saw the skeletons of resilience. The scars of conflict were fresh. I still vividly remember bullet-ridden buildings in Beira, multitudes of UN vehicles whizzing by, and graffiti reading "a luta continua" sprayed around town. That translates to "the struggle continues" and is a saying I use to this day. I realized that the issues we face are interconnected within a larger global story. This insight strengthened my passion for international relations and development, as well as my drive to fight injustice and create positive change.

That trip didn't just teach me international relations; it sank the continent into my bones. I fell in unconditional love. The music, the markets, and the resilience I witnessed became the blueprint for my life's work. By the time I headed back to the bus stop for my final commute through Harare, something in me had shifted. I was no longer just studying the world; I was already in it. My future had expanded, and for the first time, the horizon felt limitless.

Upon my return to Syracuse, it was my final semester, and I graduated from the esteemed Maxwell School of Citizenship and Public Affairs with my bachelor's degree.

On the day of my graduation, the Carrier Dome pulsed with exhilarating, infectious joy. I sensed its rhythm deep within before I heard it, a broad, resonant hum from thousands of feet stomping on the metal bleachers. Around us, caps tilted, and tassels swung silently in a dance. Families cheered loudly, their voices swelling and receding like a wave. Cameras flashed, brief bursts of light trying to capture a moment that seemed too vast to contain.

For years, I chased a dream, working hard yet smart. As I sat in that black gown, with the crowd's rhythmic noise in my ears, I realized the chase was over. I wasn't waiting for a crown; I already wore it. My crown: not made of gold, but forged in fire through countless sleepless nights and textbook pages. Graduating was a victory I built myself, trial by trial, brick by brick. I was the first in my immediate family to graduate from a 4-year university and earn my bachelor's degree. I was proud of myself.

The dean's voice echoed through the Dome. His speech followed a typical pattern for such occasions. "Today," he said, "you carry not only your personal ambitions but also the hopes of families and communities that supported you. You are proof that effort pays off and that actively pursuing dreams gives them meaning."

I looked down at my classmates' row, a line of graduates in black gowns. I noticed a girl wearing a red-and-white sash, her head bowed as she dabbed her eyes with a tissue. Next to her, a young man pressed his lips together, his jaw clenched, trying to contain a flood of emotion. We were the highlights of the ceremony, proof that hardship could become a shining, lasting achievement. For many of us, children of single parents and immigrants carrying our families' hopes, this moment meant more than just a degree. It represented both a new beginning and a sense of closure.

I thought back to all the nights I fell asleep on my textbooks, and the mornings I dragged myself to class half-asleep. This degree was more than a credential; it was a fight I had carried alone. Every financial aid loan form was mine to fill out, and I was disappointed when they offered more loans than anything else. I bought my own books and paid my way, bearing the weight of each semester. I looked around and knew some students had parents managing these details, but I was thankful, and at that moment, none of that mattered. We had made it. We were carriers of dreams, bearers of hope, makers of our own futures.

When my name was called, I rose. I smoothed the gown that brushed my ankles. I began the slow walk to the stage. Each step was heavy, not from fear but from the burden of everything that brought me here: Mom's double shifts, cold bus rides, unanswered questions, and lonely tears I kept inside. All of it followed me along that narrow aisle, a quiet march of sacrifice and triumph.

In the end, I realized my crown belonged to me. It wasn't borrowed, it wasn't begged for, and it wasn't a fleeting gift of someone else's attention. I earned this crown through my own persistent effort. The most meaningful applause wasn't the loud cheers at the Carrier Dome, but the steady joy in my heart. That joy struck me so suddenly it caught in my throat, and my body wasn't sure how to release it. With each step onstage, I understood that the applause I'd been seeking all my life had to come from within me.

I ascended the steps, and the Dome's lights grew sharper as the applause grew louder. I reached out my hand to the Dean, whose grip was firm and formal. We held on to that handshake for the official photo with the degree in my other hand, and I felt like a rockstar.

I looked ahead, eyes adjusting to the sea of faces as the stage lights blurred the crowd, until one sound rose above all the rest. A voice, sharp as a bell and impossible to mistake: my sister Nancy, shouting as loud as she could, "That's our girl! She did her thang!" Her words echoed across the Dome, drawing laughter and applause in their wake.

I turned my head, and there they all were: Mom in her finest dress, jaw clenched but eyes shining with pride she couldn't hide. For once, there was no mistaking her pride. It radiated from her seat, unmistakable and undeniable. My aunts were on their feet, shouting and waving, their pride so unashamed that it made me blush. We all squeezed together, and my cousin's camera flashed. They had shown up in large numbers, and it was clearly a significant moment, not just for me but for the entire family.

Still, out of habit, my eyes searched the crowd for my dad. I told myself not to, but I did it anyway. I scanned the bleachers for a face I hadn't seen in years, the man who once lifted me onto his shoulders and walked away without looking back. Some part of me knew better, but a stubborn corner of my heart still hoped. Maybe today would be the day. I had heard stories of fathers who returned when their children succeeded. Perhaps mine would slip in quietly, sit off to the side, and let pride do what love had never done.

I pictured him there, arms crossed, giving the silent nod of fathers in my mind, the one that said, *That's my girl.* But when I looked down the rows, there was nothing. Just the same emptiness I had known since I was four. The seat was empty, just as it had been at every recital, every ceremony, every small moment when I searched for him. Although a faint ache from his absence lingered, this time the longing didn't stop me from savoring the moment's happiness.

The applause motivated me to keep going, louder than the silence of any empty chair. For the first time, I allowed that seat to stay empty, keeping it in the past where it belonged. He had chosen to walk away; that was his decision, not mine.

You're enough, Jen, I whispered to myself. *You've always been enough. You did this without him, and you'll still be okay without him.*

I redirected my gaze toward the stage. With every step down the aisle, I was no longer walking toward a shadow. I was walking toward the girl I had envisioned for so long, the one I imagined standing tall, degree in hand, proof that she had made it. Each step drew me closer, closing the distance between the girl waiting by the doors that never opened and the woman who no longer needed them. I was no longer just "Jenny from the block," as my friend Lee affectionately calls me. I was a graduate of Syracuse University's prestigious Maxwell School with a Bachelor of Arts in International Relations.

By the time I stepped down from the stage, degree in hand, I realized something the little girl inside me had never quite believed: you don't have to be chosen by anyone else in the physical sense. You can choose yourself and bet on God. And I had been choosing and winning all along. With every step, I wasn't just walking across a stage. I was rising. I was keeping on. I was building a life not on waiting for someone else to open the door, but on what I could create with my own two hands. I was choosing.

For a brief moment, I thought this was the finish line, that the world, recognizing this parchment, would open its doors wide. I was ready to make a difference, to return to Africa, and to create the change I once envisioned there. This degree was the key to everything. At least that's what my 20-year-old self thought.

Outside, the Syracuse sun warmed the air, thick with the chatter of families and the frantic click of cameras. My family gathered around me, their faces transformed by a pride that didn't require a ritual to summon. Nancy pulled me into a hug so tight I felt it in my ribs.

On the ride back home, the very place I had worked so hard to leave behind, the degree rested on my lap, heavier than it looked. I traced the university's raised seal and thought of the counselor who had laughed and the mother who had commanded "real work." I had given them the "Medicine, Law, or Engineering" path they demanded, but I had found my own way to walk it.

The world felt ready for me to conquer it. I looked out the window at the passing highway, clutching that symbol of possibility. I didn't know then that more challenges lay ahead, but it didn't matter.

For those few fleeting minutes, I felt the world unlock its doors, clearing the path for the life I had finally chosen for myself.

Tracie and I on our graduation day at Syracuse University in 1994.

Chapter Four

STANDING AT THE CROSSROADS

By the time I turned twenty, most people saw me as having already achieved my goals by living life by the book. I had been the perfect student. I skipped eighth grade, aced advanced classes, and graduated from high school at sixteen. I walked across the stage at Syracuse before my twenty-first birthday with a stellar record. For years, teachers praised me as the one who lived up to the promise, making me a role model for lower-classmen. So, what could go wrong?

I carried a pocketful of maxims I believed were universal truths: "Good things come to those who wait," "What goes around comes around," and "Hard work beats talent when talent doesn't work hard." One of my favorites was "When one door closes, multiple windows open."

After graduation, I had hoped my surroundings would reflect my success. Instead, I traded the intellectual fire of Syracuse for the familiar dampness of my aunt's basement.

While I was away, my mother and sister had moved to Long Island, into a space barely large enough for the two of them. The ceiling was so low I could almost touch it. Once again, my mother, my sister, and I were living under someone else's roof.

The mismatch was dizzying. Just months earlier, I had been in Zimbabwe, Zambia, and Mozambique, debating international policy with scholars and navigating the complexities of a continent in transition. Now I was back on the pavement of New York.

It wasn't the launchpad I'd imagined; it was an underground bunker. Some days, it felt like all those late nights and long years at Syracuse had only taken me back to the bottom. But despite the low ceilings of the basement and the uncertainty of my career, there was the undeniable joy of being back among my own.

I have always been fiercely loyal to community and friendships. I'm the kind of woman who doesn't forget where she came from or the people who walked the first miles with her. I was genuinely glad to reconnect with old friends and family, to feel the rhythm of the city, and to step back into the lives of those I'd left behind.

One friend I had been looking forward to connecting with more than anyone else was Javon.

I first met Javon in sixth grade back in Hollis. One day, he looked at my notebook and said, "You've got nice handwriting. You should write my rhymes down." Those few words hit me like a crown on my head. For a moment, I felt like somebody's princess. I felt seen, chosen, and worthy. I had never received that kind of attention before, and perhaps that is why I clung to it for so long.

I remember thinking, *This boy sees me.* He saw the girl who could make words sing, not just a chubby nerd. In return, I saw a boy who could be a star if someone just believed in him. I looked at him and thought he was cool and going to be somebody. We became instant friends.

Javon was a boy with a big laugh and a soft heart, even though circumstances never gave him a soft place to land. After his parents split up early in their relationship, he grew up split between his parents' places and his grandparents' home in Hollis. His father was in a wheelchair and battled addiction until he eventually overdosed in Brooklyn. With his father gone, the streets became Javon's second parent. Music was his only escape. He could freestyle for five minutes straight without a hook or a breath, telling stories about eviction notices and corner-store legends.

Between the letters we exchanged while I was at Syracuse and our reunion in Queens after graduation, we somehow started dating. Being with Javon felt like living inside a movie trailer. It was a crazy, mad love. He was my shield, and in turn, the streets respected me. People would nod and say, "That's Javon's girl" when I walked by. The message was simple: Don't mess with her. He was my human protector, and he loved me without hesitation.

I didn't realize it then, but Javon wasn't just my boyfriend; he was my first project. I thought if I could just apply enough belief, enough strategy, and enough love, I could help him navigate a world that had never given him a fair shake.

However, a bachelor's degree and a complicated "project" at home do not exactly pave the way for an easy life. In fact, they created a strange friction. My inner world was full of grand theories and grander dreams, but my outer world was shrinking.

And as much as I wanted to focus on Javon, I had a more pressing project: my own survival.

Soon enough, I knew I had to find a job. My mom was still struggling to take care of herself, let alone us. She worked as a caregiver, spending most of the week in elderly clients' homes and only coming home on weekends, completely drained. I saw her giving everything she had, yet never quite breaking even.

I was determined to end that cycle and help lift us both out of that daily struggle. My mom's struggles felt like my own burden to carry. She had raised us through so much yet still had not found rest.

One by one, I started applying for jobs, carefully examining each listing to find one that matched my skills. I searched for terms like "global development" and "public policy," only to realize I was still somehow underqualified. Since I was no stranger to rejection, I kept trying, convinced that every door that closed was guiding me toward the one meant for me. I knocked again and again, but still, nothing opened.

The hardest part was running into some of my former classmates. They all seemed to be settling into their next chapter, dressed in office clothes and moving to new cities. They had graduate program acceptances and job offers in hand, not just from their resumes but also from parents and uncles pulling strings. I smiled and congratulated them, but inside I felt the pain of being first-generation. I didn't have an uncle at a law firm or a family friend to slip my resume into the right pile. It was just me, my loans, and the undeniable truth that while others walk through open doors, I would have to keep knocking harder and longer to squeeze in.

Soon, my job search shifted toward roles such as "Administrative Assistant," "Office Clerk," and "Data Entry." My dreams of shaping global policy recessed into work that felt monotonous. How could someone like me, who did well in school and was destined for great things, end up here, knocking on doors that didn't seem to hold promise?

I finally signed up with a temp agency, and my first job was at McKinsey as an Executive Assistant in a windowless Manhattan cubicle. The hum of the copier and the phone ringing were my background noise. I wore the same blazer three times a week, feeling like an impostor. I daydreamed of drafting policy memos for the State Department, only to have my peace shattered by another friendly salesperson calling for our fax number.

The paycheck was decent; however, most of it went toward loan payments, barely making a dent in my debt. Each month, I signed checks with a knot in my stomach, haunted by my mother's struggle to stretch a dollar to cover three meals. I promised never to live that way, but I was stuck in the cycle at the time.

It didn't take long to realize that my bachelor's degree wasn't a golden ticket; it was merely a first step in the world of qualifications.

The jobs I had dreamed of in international affairs went to people with master's degrees. Out of desperation and determination, I began researching graduate programs.

I applied to several schools and ultimately enrolled at American University in Washington, D.C. I focused on Comparative and Regional Studies, with an emphasis on Africa. I also took public health courses at George Washington University as a minor to connect the dots between politics, development, and health. On the one hand, it was a silver lining, or perhaps a trap. I qualified for another student loan, which meant I could put the old one on hold until I finished my studies. It bought me time, but it also pushed me further into the debt I was trying to escape.

I packed my bags, left New York, and arrived in Maryland, where the cost of living was lower. I rented an apartment in Silver Spring with help from my student loan. Unlike undergrad, graduate school didn't include dorms or meal plans. You were an adult now, at least on paper. I told myself that graduate school wasn't just about earning more credentials; it was about buying time to find my way.

The apartment was a modest two-bedroom place in a nice neighborhood. For a while, I had a roommate whose face I can no longer recall. Eventually, she moved out, and my sister decided to come down from New York to be with me. That marked the beginning of my family's migration to the South.

My graduate studies were supposed to take two years, but for me they stretched into three. The luxury of being a full-time student was out of reach. Fortunately, graduate programs were designed for working individuals, with classes held in the evenings. But that didn't make the days any shorter. I worked full-time while studying full-time. By the time I finally headed home, it was often close to ten at night or later.

During that busy time, I discovered community. The Black Graduate Student Association at American University became a vital support network for me. When I came across the organization, it was dormant. I took the initiative to revive it, along with friends like Evita, who was from Louisiana and loved cats. I became the President and built the community I needed. Like Syracuse, American University was predominantly White, and as graduate students, most of us were spread across the city, juggling jobs, classes, and bills. Still, we created our own space. It was another great chance to take on a leadership role.

I spent one of my spring breaks exploring London and Paris, my first time ever in Europe. These were places I'd only ever seen in books or movies. Standing in front of the Louvre or looking up at Big Ben, I started thinking about those 'imagined communities' I'd read about in class. It was wild to realize how I already felt a connection to these distant landmarks and the history they represented, even though I was a girl from Queens who had never stepped foot on the continent before. It made the world feel smaller and more connected all at once. But as I stared at those towering monuments, I realized they weren't just landmarks. They were deliberate claims on the land, built by people who wanted to make sure their story was the only one that survived. It made me wonder who gets to decide which stories become stone and which ones are left to blow away in the wind.

When I wasn't crossing oceans, I was finding my way across the States. I explored California wine country or took a quick trip to Virginia Beach with friends like Anissa, who hailed from the big ole state of Texas. She is still the self-proclaimed "president of the Jen Erie Fan Club." You have to love friends like that.

Those escapes brought absolute joy, but they sat alongside the grind of temp jobs and night classes, long train rides with a textbook on my lap, and evenings spent counting crumpled bills to make rent.

Without even realizing it, studying at American University in the nation's capital placed me so close to the center of world power. One professor left a lasting impression: Dr. Fantu Cheru, an Ethiopian scholar who challenged conventional thinking about international development. As an economist, he wouldn't let us see Africa as a place to be rescued. He framed it as a continent of complexity and vast potential. I can still hear him saying: "Don't come with answers. Come with questions. Development is not charity; it's justice. And if you're serious, you have to be willing to do the hard work."

Sitting in Dr. Cheru's lectures, I realized he wasn't just teaching theory. Every late night, every loan, and every paper had to add up to something bigger than just getting by.

Another meaningful experience was my required internship for the public health program. I became a certified HIV and STI counselor at Whitman-Walker's Max Robinson Center in the heart of Southeast Washington, D.C. I appreciated the clinic's team and the clients who entrusted me with such responsibility. It was my first exposure to the multi-layered complexities of human behavior and societal access. Although it was an unpaid position, the experience solidified my passion for public health.

As I neared the end of my program, several of us, including Anissa, decided to take the State Department Foreign Service exam. The State Department was our Golden Gate. If we passed, we would enter a career with purpose, prestige, and security.

I dressed carefully for the test, wearing my best navy skirt suit and a pair of simple pearl earrings. I wanted the examiners to see me as someone who belonged there.

When it was time to enter the room, sweat and anxiety got the best of me. My posture shifted from that of a confident diplomat back to that of just a girl from Queens. I gave it my all, but when the results came in, I had failed miserably. So had nearly everyone else I knew. At first, I laughed, but deep down I felt a mix of shame and the suspicion that the system wasn't set up for people like us.

That day changed everything. It was one of the most painful rejections I've ever faced. I kept asking myself, "How much more do I have to prove?"

That night, I locked myself in my room and cried like a baby. It was exhausting to work so hard and still find every door bolted.

In the middle of that professional wreckage, I realized there was one more thing I had to let go of. When I left for D.C., Javon and I tried the long-distance thing with calls and letters. But the truth was, we had become worlds apart. I was filling out financial aid forms; he was filling out plea deals. I was learning to pronounce hegemony; he was learning the difference between county and state time. Even on breaks, sharing a chopped cheese sandwich at our old bodega, his stories no longer fit inside my mouth.

The letters kept coming. His handwriting was surprisingly neat, quoting Lauryn Hill and asking for pictures. Even though he had been out for a while, I still lived in fear of seeing a state prison return address in my mailbox again. I kept them in a Nike shoebox under my bed, but with each new envelope, the connection thinned.

I remember one letter in particular. I had written to him in a moment of total vulnerability, pouring out the pain of the Foreign Service rejection and the crushing weight of feeling "not enough" for the world I was trying to enter. I needed a partner to help me carry the grief. Instead, his response was a single, familiar refrain:

"I love you, baby, it will be ok, can't wait to see you."

I held the letter until the heat of my hands blurred the ink. It was a hollow sentence, a placeholder for a future that would never arrive. In that moment, the mismatch became a chasm. I was talking about global policy and the shattering of my professional dreams; he was still stuck in a cycle of promises.

Once, his attention felt like a crown on my head. Now, those same words felt like rocks. They were anchoring me to a version of myself I had outgrown. I looked at his neat handwriting and finally whispered into the darkness, "I can't fix him."

I realized then that by trying to "save" him, I was actually drowning myself. That day, I finally gave myself permission to let him go, but it felt like a betrayal of the highest order.

As I grieved the professional rejections, I found myself submerged in a second layer of grief. I realized I wasn't just mourning Javon. I was releasing a lie I had held for years, the one that kept me from facing the truth about the first man who left and never looked back. In my mind, I saw the little girl I once was. She stood at the door with uneven pigtails and untied sneakers, waiting for my father to return with a carton of milk and call me his princess.

But as I looked at that little girl, I also saw Javon. I saw the boy whose father had overdosed while in a wheelchair, the boy who had been thrown into the deep end of the streets before he even knew how to swim. He was a product of every door that had ever been slammed in his face. Now, here I was, the person who claimed to love him most, preparing to slam one more door.

I was torn apart by the cruelty of it. How could I judge him for being a "project" when he was just a man trying to survive a system designed to break him? If I left him now, would he break and end up behind bars again? Wasn't I just proving that he was as disposable as the world had told him he was?

I sat there in the dark, the letter from Javon still warm in my hand. I felt like a hypocrite. I was out here fighting for "global justice" and "human rights" in my graduate seminars, yet I was about to abandon a man who had been denied both since the day he was born. I loved him, but I was beginning to understand a terrifying truth: you can love someone with your whole heart and still not have enough room in your life for their chaos.

I cried for the four-year-old who was never lifted into the air again, but I also cried for Javon because I knew that by choosing my own life, I was leaving him in the water. I was swimming for the shore, and I couldn't carry him on my back anymore.

As the sobs slowed, I felt the little girl in pigtails finally loosen her grip. I realized the man she longed for wasn't in Javon. He wasn't in anyone. He was gone. The only person who could tend to that wound was the woman now standing in the place of that little girl. It was the most selfish and the most necessary thing I have ever done. I chose myself, but the cost was leaving a piece of my soul behind in Queens.

Life doesn't give you much time for epiphanies when you have bills to pay. Amid my grief, I had to keep moving. To make matters worse, my nine-month work contract ended, and I suddenly found myself unemployed. I headed back into the job market, now armed with a master's degree, thinking the hardest part was over.

Instead, I received the same answer repeatedly: "No. Not enough." Then came the plot twist: "But of course, for even our entry-level posts, we require two years of overseas field experience."

I felt the world was playing a rigged game. I had shed the shackles of my past, but the doors of my future were still locked. I'd spent my whole life scared of ending up like my mom, living paycheck to paycheck, but now I didn't even have a paycheck. I was better educated than she was, but I had managed to sink even lower into the trap.

After several more rejections, I was done trying to solve the puzzle on my own. I turned to those who had already made it, approaching several leaders in the NGO space for informational interviews. I sat in polished offices across from executives at international nonprofits, people who were thriving in the world I so desperately wanted to inhabit.

Frankly, I hoped one of them would be my miracle. With every meeting, a part of me waited for someone to say, "Don't worry, I'll make a phone call," or "Let me talk to my people," or even, "Come see me at my office on Monday." I wanted someone to be the uncle or the family friend I didn't have, the one who would finally slip my resume into the right pile.

Instead, the answer was always the same. I would sit there and ask, "What am I missing? I've studied, I've worked hard, and I've done everything by the book. Why can't I break in?"

They would look at me with varying degrees of pity and say, "You've got to understand. This work doesn't have one door. It's a hallway of locked doors. A degree gets you into the hallway, but it won't get you through. You need more keys, field experience, connections, and persistence."

I would lean in, my voice tense with the frustration of a woman already exhausted. "But how am I supposed to gain experience if no one will give me the chance?"

The advice inevitably circled back to one thing. "That's exactly why so many of us volunteer overseas, usually with the Peace Corps. Have you ever considered that?"

I would frown. The idea felt like a step backward, not forward. "Peace Corps? It feels like covert government work. And to go live in a mud hut in some far-flung country for free? I'm just not sure."

They would smile knowingly, offering the same hard truth. "The Peace Corps could really be your ticket. Two years abroad, working in real communities and learning new languages, is the only way organizations will take you seriously."

The Peace Corps wasn't the dream I was chasing. It felt like a detour, a pause I couldn't afford. The prospect of two years without a salary, coupled with the debt already pressing in, forced me to confront a question I had managed to avoid until then. How do you choose service when survival is still undecided?

Taking in the sights during a quick getaway to Paris.

Chapter Five

MY PEACE CORPS JOURNEY

The answer to that question didn't come in a flash of inspiration. It came in the form of a long, quiet stare at my bank account. I realized that if I stayed where I was, survival would always be a question. If I left, I would be answering it on my own terms.

With newfound clarity, I applied to the Peace Corps, treating the application like a life raft rather than a gap year. I went through the interviews and shared my goals with the agency with total transparency. Things looked promising, and I allowed myself to start dreaming again.

I had a very specific vision for my volunteer life abroad. I wanted to be in a Francophone country, preferably in West Africa, where I could discover my roots and learn French fluently. Growing up with Haitian Creole, I felt a magnetic pull toward that heritage.

When the recruiter finally called, my palms were sweaty. I was ready to hear the name of a country like Senegal or Benin.

"We have good news and bad news," the recruiter said.

I braced myself and felt my stomach churn. *Was I about to be rejected all over again?*

"The bad news is that the West Africa cohort has been postponed indefinitely, or at least for six months."

My mind was reeling. I pressed my hand to my forehead, convinced I must have misheard. I could not wait that long.

"Well," she continued, "the good news is we have openings for South Africa. You could leave right away. It is one of our newest programs, and you would be part of the third group we are sending there."

"South Africa?!," I said in shock.

That was not the plan. I was supposed to be learning French and tracing my ancestors' path. More than that, I was afraid. It was 1998, and the world was still watching the fragile, bloody transition of a country that had just escaped apartheid. When I heard the words "South Africa," my mind didn't think of "roots." It thought of racism, violence, and a deep, systemic anger that had only just begun to simmer. Was it truly safe for me to go there, especially as a Black person?

"You don't have to decide right now," she said. "But if you want to leave soon, this is the only option available."

I hung up the phone with a frown and knots in my stomach. Sitting on the edge of my bed, I looked at the boxes stacked in the corner, half-packed, where they'd been for days.

I faced a dilemma between two fears. I was afraid of South Africa's unpredictable violence, yet I was more frightened by the stagnation of my current life. Six more months of temporary jobs was a cost I couldn't afford.

At that moment, the "detour" became the destination. I realized the Peace Corps wasn't just about service; it was about moving on to somewhere else. Anywhere. Even toward a place that scared me.

In January 1999, forty of us left the orientation program in Philadelphia and touched down in Johannesburg. For decades, the

Peace Corps had been geared toward a specific kind of volunteer, and that person usually didn't look like me. But in the spirit of the new South African "Rainbow Nation," our cohort was a mirror of that dream. In those early days, the Peace Corps ensured the groups they sent out were a mix of Black, Asian, Indian, and Latino Americans. They were the most diverse groups the agency had ever assembled, the American melting pot.

We didn't stay in Johannesburg long. They loaded us onto a bus headed to the Peace Corps office in Pretoria, and I spent the drive staring out the window, trying to reconcile the South Africa I had seen on the news with the one passing by. I expected to see a country in the middle of a visible, raw transition. Instead, as we pulled into Pretoria, everything looked unnervingly quiet yet understatedly beautiful.

As we passed by the Union Buildings, I thought of Nelson Mandela, about the long, brutal struggle he and his comrades endured to confront injustice, and how, even in the darkest of hours, he resisted and never gave up. His legacy, and that of Winnie too, continues to inspire millions to believe in dignity, resilience, and the possibility of change.

It was summer time and the heat pressed against the bus windows, thick and unmoving, the kind that settles into your skin. Outside, the city passed in shades of deep green and sun-faded earth, trees heavy with leaves, their branches stretching wide over broad avenues. Bougainvillea burst over concrete walls in defiant reds and pinks, and the sidewalks were buzzing with activity between foot traffic and vendors selling everything you could think of. It felt uncannily familiar. The quiet order of the suburbs, the manicured gardens, even the way time seemed to move a little slower reminded me of Harare, beautiful, composed, and seemingly holding its breath. Yet here too, every home was shielded behind high walls and electric fencing, a reminder that beauty here lived side by side with vigilance.

The Peace Corps kept us on a tight leash. Staff herded us from the bus directly into a hostel, issuing stern warnings against wandering too far. For the next few days, we sat through endless safety briefings and flipped through thick packets of warnings. They talked about carjackings, health risks, and security protocols until I stopped looking at the trees and started looking over my shoulder. We moved everywhere in a pack.

Part of our orientation included intensive language training. My assignment was Sepedi, the language spoken in the Northern Province, which was later renamed Limpopo.

After finishing our check-in in Pretoria, we moved to a training center in Tzaneen. It was one of the most beautiful places I had ever seen. We were surrounded by lush green hills, tea fields, and fruit farms heavy with my favorite mangoes and oranges. It felt heavenly.

But the dream was about to become very real.

Our training included a two-week homestay with a local family. For the first time, we wouldn't be traveling as a protected group. We were placed solo to practice our still-forming language skills with real South Africans. The Peace Corps stationed me in a small town called Botlokwa. Try saying that 3x fast. It sure was a mouthful, and I still butcher it to this day.

I met my host family on the first day: a mother, a father, and two young daughters. This household lived the reality of the migrant labor system every day. The father was mostly away, working in a Johannesburg gold mine to support the family, while the mother ran the household. Their home was modest but welcoming. It had a main building with four small rooms, a separate kitchen structure, and a latrine out back.

The mother and daughters were so lovely and welcoming. They tried their best to speak to me in their limited English, just as I tried to use my limited Sepedi. One daughter slept with her mother, while I shared a room with the other daughter. The room was simple, with just two single beds, but it was comfortable.

My biggest challenge and fear was using the bathroom, a pit latrine in an outhouse in the backyard that felt like a mile from the main house. I had to learn the best squatting position quickly while dodging as many flies and spiders as possible. It was one of my worst first experiences of living in a rural environment. But there was nothing I could do about it, so I had to get used to it and keep moving. Plus, it was only for two weeks. How much worse could it really be?

South Africa had an answer for me.

One morning, I opened the door to my room, ready to head outside to the kitchen for breakfast. Thank God for the slow pace of village life, I paused. I glanced down after I opened the back door, just before my foot hit the ground. That pause saved me. A long, vibrant green snake lay stretched across the entrance, as if it were decorative trim.

I froze. Then I did exactly what any city girl would do: I screamed as if the world were ending. My voice probably echoed across the entire valley. Within seconds, a neighbor arrived. He looked as calm as if he were going to check the mail. He didn't even flinch. He grabbed a shovel and, with one clean swing, took the snake's head off as if he were swatting a fly.

"Don't worry," he shrugged. "It happens."

He walked away, leaving me trembling. By the time my heart stopped racing, the village was back to business, quietly chuckling at my Broadway-level performance. For them, a snake was a Tuesday morning chore. For me, it was pure terror.

For the rest of that stay, I slept with one eye open every night. Can you blame me? I was living in a place where deadly spiders watched you in the bathroom, and snakes didn't just cross paths through the yard; they took naps right on your doorstep.

After surviving the homestay, we reconvened in Tzaneen to wrap up our training. The time had finally come to head into the remote communities that would be our homes for the next two years.

From a distance, I saw a white single-cab pickup truck pull up in front of the center. One of the Peace Corps staff pointed toward it. "Jen, that is the ride to your future," he said.

A short, elderly, well-dressed woman jumped out of the

passenger side. She looked me up and down behind her eyeglasses and spoke in a sharp, clear voice.

"Dumela, Jen," she said in Sepedi, smiling at me.

"Dumela, Mme," I responded. I felt a surge of pride at being able to answer her with confidence.

She nodded, seemingly satisfied. "Leina la ka ke Mme Maraba," she continued. She explained that she was the head principal of the school where I would be working and that I would be living in her home.

Once we tossed my bags into the back, Mme Maraba gestured toward the truck.

"Sepela," she said, pointing to the cab. "Let's go."

I climbed into the front seat, but it was a very snug fit. I was wedged tightly between the driver and the gearshift on one side, and my new host mother and supervisor on the other. Every time the driver shifted gears, I had to move my knees to make room.

"Two hours," the driver said, looking at me with a small grin as he started the engine.

I settled in as best I could. The ride felt endless, but the savannah and rolling hills around us offered a quiet kind of beauty that held my attention.

We finally arrived in a township called Mahwelereng, the place I would come to call home.

At first, I felt completely lonely and isolated, even though I shared a house with a host family and worked with four different schools. It was the first time I had been so far from home in a completely unfamiliar country for such a long period alone. I felt scared and miserably homesick, often crying myself to sleep at night.

I found comfort in going to the neighborhood Telkom phone shop. I would wait in line at the container, sometimes for an hour or more, just for the chance to connect with my mother and Nancy back home.

Not surprisingly, my mother would always remind me that I could quit my "silly experiment" and move back to the US at any time. Nancy, on the other hand, would reassure me that I just needed to give it more time and that I was exactly where I was supposed to be.

One mid-morning, I stood on a concrete platform in front of a row of low-slung school buildings for assembly. Below me, hundreds of children stood in rows so straight they looked like miniature soldiers. I saw pride and poverty in equal measure: freshly pressed trousers and polished shoes, but also tears patched and laces frayed.

As I stood there, wondering if the heat would ever break, the children began to sing Nkosi Sikelel' iAfrika, South Africa's national anthem.

The sound took me by surprise. Their voices blended, strong and clear, carrying the melody across the dusty yard. One verse melted into another, in Xhosa, Sesotho, Zulu, Afrikaans, and English. As they reached the final lines, I understood every word: "Sounds the call to come together, and united we shall stand." The purity of their voices in that schoolyard moved me to my core. Suddenly, the heat on my skin and the ache of missing home faded into the background.

The principal stepped forward to introduce me in Sepedi, and hundreds of eyes turned toward me. At university, I had been president of a student organization, standing confidently before thousands. Yet here, I felt my heart hammer against my ribs under the gaze of primary schoolers.

Then a teacher called out, and the children began clapping in a perfect, rhythmic chant.

"Thaaaank you, Miss Jenneeeeefer!"

Clap. Clap-clap. Clap.

"Wellllcome to Lim-po-po!"

I couldn't help but laugh. It was vibrant, musical, and entirely different from the polite applause back home. With each clap, the tension inside me melted away. I finally breathed freely. For the first time since landing in South Africa, I didn't feel like a girl suspended between uncertainty and doubt. I felt like I belonged.

65

That morning was the first of many. I eventually rotated through four schools, where each assembly greeted me with its own distinct blend of order, ritual, and song. Each time, I felt honored and a bit overwhelmed. Seeing the hopeful faces of the new generation meant to carry South Africa forward was both humbling and a heavy responsibility.

One school had a computer lab. The volunteer before me, a guy named Ro from Chicago, had secured a donation of about twenty computers, but he left just as they arrived. I stepped in at exactly the right time and helped set up the lab. Soon, I was teaching basic computer skills, starting with turning on a machine, typing, and using a mouse. For many students, and even some teachers, it was their first time touching a computer.

While the lab felt like progress, my primary assignment was much more complicated. I was officially assigned to four primary schools to train teachers. South Africa had just introduced a new curriculum called Outcomes-Based Education, or OBE. I was not a certified teacher, but because I had grown up with OBE in the States, the Peace Corps believed I could help demystify it. Every day, I would ride my bicycle to each school until I figured out a rotation schedule.

Suddenly, the "honor" I felt at the assemblies met the reality of the staff room. I found myself standing before teachers twice my age, pushing group work and 'learner-centered' theories on professionals who had spent decades teaching with nothing but a chalkboard and a stick.

There were days when I felt like a total fraud. Who was I to tell experienced educators how to run their classrooms? I had two degrees but no teaching certificate. Some teachers strongly opposed the idea of being taught by a child. They would gripe in the break room and roll their eyes whenever I launched a workshop. To them, change felt like a personal attack.

But even as some rolled their eyes, others still looked to me as the "expert" from America and often asked me for extra help in the classroom.

I remember one day sitting in a Grade 6 classroom, notebook in hand. The teacher asked me to help grade a set of tests. I sat at his desk, reviewing the answers with a red pen. Some kids had done beautifully. Others had clearly done their best in the worst possible way, filling the page with earnest guesses that didn't quite hit the mark.

Once I finished the last script, the teacher gathered the students at the front. I thought he was going to review the answers. Instead, he lined them up. The teacher singled out the perfect scores, sending them back to their desks while the rest remained standing, silent and stiff. Only then did I realize that my red ink had just sealed their fate.

One by one, the teacher ordered them forward. The first boy, no older than eleven, braced himself against the edge of a desk. The stick came down hard across his back. He flinched but stayed silent. The next child stepped up, knowing that two mistakes meant two lashes. By the time the last few stood there trembling, I could barely breathe. My throat constricted. I wanted to grab the stick and yell that this was wrong. Instead, tears clouded my vision, and I stumbled out before I completely broke down.

I ran straight to the headmistress's office. "How can this happen? Corporal punishment is banned!" My voice cracked with anger.

She looked at me calmly, almost wearily. "Yes, it is banned. But parents expect it. They tell us that if we don't discipline their children, we aren't doing our job."

I became an advocate for those children. Before long, every teacher knew that beating children upset Jen. When I entered a classroom, the sticks would vanish, slipped under desks or tucked behind cupboards. But I knew the sticks would come out again the moment I left.

The incident with the stick changed everything for me. I couldn't be a passive observer anymore. I began to see that the "discipline" in the schools was often just a lid on a boiling pot of issues no one wanted to talk about. While teachers focused on punishing kids for their test scores, a much more dangerous threat was unfolding outside the classroom walls. In this community, nearly everyone had lost someone to AIDS.

Beyond training teachers on the curriculum, the Peace Corps also assigned me to work on community health outreach, which meant stepping directly into the path of a storm.

HIV and AIDS were ripping through the country like wildfire, claiming many community members: parents, children, teachers, police officers, and more. However, back then, nobody really talked about it. It was heavily stigmatized, and the cause of death was often listed as an opportunistic infection, such as tuberculosis or "slimming disease," whatever that was. That was the most acceptable and least shameful explanation for families.

By 1999, the virus had spread to nearly every home. More than one in ten adults was living with HIV, and in some parts of Limpopo, the numbers were even higher. During that time, I worked closely with local NGOs, including the Planned Parenthood Federation of South Africa, the Red Cross Society, and LoveLife. Our main goal was to educate young people, reaching them before they were exposed to misinformation or risk. We visited high schools, organized community events, led sessions at health clinics, and sometimes stayed late to run workshops using flip charts and posters.

In addition to these efforts, I also worked at one of the local youth-designated clinics. Students would come after school to take tests for HIV, other STIs, or pregnancy. They would attend our health talks there. We'd have games for them to play to help them open up to us. We'd talk about reproductive health, the dual protection of condoms, and the pros and cons of other family planning products like injectables. We emphasized delaying sex if possible and dealing with peer pressure.

One afternoon, I was in a classroom led by a teacher who had become a friend. I decided to pivot from our usual lesson to discuss reproductive health and STIs. As soon as I mentioned the word "condom," the air in the room shifted. The teacher, usually so friendly, stood up and walked toward me, her face tight.

"Jennifer, stop," she whispered, loud enough for the front row to hear. "We do not discuss these matters here. It is not our way."

I tried to explain that these kids were already at risk, but she wouldn't hear it.

"In this school, we teach," she said, her voice like iron. "We do not 'corrupt.' Stick to the curriculum and leave the rest alone."

The school system became my two-front battleground. On one side, I fought to change how they taught; on the other, I fought a silent war against a disease that the administration refused to name. I grew passionate about maternal health and HIV education, even though I was blocked at every turn by the very people charged with protecting these children. At one school, the staff nearly staged a revolt when they learned we were planning to distribute condoms.

Nevertheless, our work had to continue. We still had to go to schools, community centers, and clinics. We pressed on despite the resistance and challenges. Each time, I reminded myself that I had spent years studying to make a difference in these communities. Yes, I had come to this place to volunteer and gain experience in international development, but for me, this was not just another box-ticking exercise. If I couldn't make a difference, then what was the point?

Sometimes, we had to get creative by telling young people to find us at the local clinic. We had to avoid upsetting community members and school leaders who, in trying to protect students by withholding information, were actually leaving them to dangerous self-interpretation.

These students were fiercely curious. They came to us after school, some privately, asking endless questions about biology, relationships, and risks. It quickly became clear that information alone wasn't enough; they needed guidance, support, and an advocate. In those moments, I saw the limits of what we could do. While I was busy handing out pamphlets and teaching biology, some students were already navigating dangerous situations that no amount of classroom guidance could instantly fix. Poverty added another layer of complexity. Older men, sometimes called sugar daddies or blessers, waited near school gates, offering small gifts or money to girls in exchange for favors. Many of these young women were not making these choices freely; they were fighting for survival in households where resources were scarce, and care responsibilities were enormous.

Outside of class, I loved spending time with the students. I had brought a small boombox radio and some cassettes from the States, and to them, it felt like magic. They would gather around as I pressed play, and the beats of Queen Latifah or Wyclef Jean would fill the Mahwelereng air. They loved hip hop just as I did. There was even a mural of Tupac, not too far from where I lived, that I passed by all the time. Some kids would try to sing along, stumbling over the words, while others would laugh and sway to the music.

Music was our common language, and for a moment, the distance between America and South Africa felt like nothing. But I soon realized that while our music traveled across the ocean, the context didn't always follow.

On days without dancing, we simply hung out on the stoop and talked. It was during one of these peaceful afternoons that the cultural gap unexpectedly caught me off guard.

A few boys came by to visit, and one of them, who couldn't have been more than eleven or twelve years old, reached out to slap my hand in greeting.

"What's up, my nig*a?" he said, grinning.

I froze. I was so shocked that my entire demeanor changed instantly. I looked at the little boy for a second, then asked him to repeat what he had just said. He repeated it without even blinking, proud. That was the first time in my life anyone had ever called me that to my face. To me, that term was nothing but vile and negative, and hearing it in this peaceful moment felt like a total violation. I looked him straight in the eye.

"That word is offensive," I told him firmly. "You should never use it again."

He looked surprised. I could tell he felt terrible because he genuinely believed he was just being cool with me.

"Where did you learn that?" I asked.

"The movies," he said. "And the music from America."

I couldn't stay mad at him for long because it wasn't his fault. The way the mainstream media portrays it, with Black people themselves using the n-word as if it's cool and hip, it's no wonder anyone thinks it's okay or even desirable. I used the situation as a teachable moment, explaining the word's negative origins and why I personally am against using it. He apologized, and we moved on. I put on some Bob Marley to smooth out the atmosphere.

Otherwise, the kids had so many questions, often making me laugh with their curiosity about America and what life was like beyond Limpopo, things they'd only seen in magazines or heard on the radio. We'd joke around and tease each other. The boys were bold and persistent in their questioning, while the girls were usually a bit shy.

But behind the laughter and jokes, I began to notice a darkness that humor couldn't fully mask. The jokes about "sugar daddies," for example, felt too harsh to be mere innocent fun; for some girls, they reflected painful choices forced on them by their circumstances. Similarly, a careless remark about a classmate who had lost both parents to AIDS revealed a sadness that was always just beneath the surface. I would catch glimpses of it in a downcast gaze, a forced smile, or the quiet effort to hold it together before their peers.

While they tried to keep it together, I would soon learn that some of the burdens these children carried were staggering. Some were raising younger siblings, some were negotiating relationships that were anything but innocent, and some were living with losses far too heavy for their age. They looked at me with curiosity, eager to know about my life in America, but I often found myself more curious about them. How did they endure? How did they still find reasons to laugh, and how did they bear so much while still moving forward? At night, alone in my room, I thought about the differences between us. I had my own wounds, such as the absence of my father, a mother caught up in her own stress, student loans, and doubts about belonging. But compared to these young people, my troubles felt minimal. They grappled with questions of survival, dignity, and whether they could truly trust anyone.

The greatest threat to that survival was the one thing no one would name. I realized that the "dignity" the community was trying to protect was actually a wall of silence surrounding the AIDS epidemic.

I used to think the worst part was what we didn't say. I was wrong. The worst part was how quickly we got used to not saying it. The silence itself was a recurring burden. I remembered funeral after funeral, where the silence was as much a part of the procession as the casket. Whether this was a cultural custom or a deep-seated fear of confronting a truth I hadn't yet uncovered, I didn't yet know. But I knew most families had already paid too much, and these young people were the ones bearing the brunt of the cost. Without breaking that silence, they would only continue to pay more.

And it wasn't just the silence at the funerals. The taboo surrounding sex and the inability to mention it created space for abuse. How could a young girl speak openly about being violated if the very language to describe the act did not exist?

It became clear to me that if I was going to be impactful, breaking that silence had to be a priority during my time there. I was grateful to have some brave allies in the community and dedicated NGO counterparts who were willing to speak up alongside me. However, it is hard to be a loud advocate for change during the day when you have to be a quiet, polite guest at night.

I lived with a few host families over the two years. My second host family, the Thlakos, was a middle-class couple with three kids, and they treated me less like a guest and more like another daughter. They integrated me into everything. If there was a wedding or a community gathering, I was right there with a plate of food in my hands. I learned the unspoken rules: never walk alone after sunset as a woman, and never linger too long.

I quickly learned that Limpopo set its own pace. No one rushed a conversation, and the clock mattered far less than the person standing right in front of you. In Queens, neighbors might not even make eye contact, but in Mahwelereng, a fifteen-minute walk to school could turn into an hour-long conversation about your mother, your father, and your health. At first, the New Yorker in me was frustrated. I would actually sprint the rest of the way to school to stay on the schedule I had set for myself.

Mme Thlako, my host mom, would just laugh at me when I came home stressed about the time. She started encouraging me to leave earlier, not so I could be "on time" for work, but so I would have plenty of time to connect with people along the way. She was determined to see me truly connected to the community, and she seemed to have her own ideas about how to make sure I never wanted to leave. She was planting seeds for a future I hadn't even considered.

This home became the place where my life would transform in ways I didn't see coming.

Officially swearing in with the Peace Corps SA3 group in 1999.

Our Peace Corps South Africa SA3 group photo during training.

Posing with my students for a final group photo before leaving South Africa in 2001.

CHAPTER SIX

LEARNING TO LIVE BEYOND THE DUTY

South Africa involved more than just tough lessons, funerals, and the work that sustained me. There were times when life broke open, allowing joy to flow in.

Sometimes that meant dancing badly to Kwaito music and laughing until my ribs hurt. Sometimes it meant loosening the armor I had relied on for survival and learning to breathe without it. I had learned to endure. South Africa, it turned out, wanted to teach me something else.

Before I arrived, I believed I needed a full closet, a stocked refrigerator, and the reassurance of an American paycheck. Living on roughly $200 a month felt reckless when I left New York. In Limpopo, it was more than enough.

We wasted nothing. A local shop mended everything, clothes, shoes, umbrellas, you name it, until there was nothing left to save. When the water cut off, we hauled buckets from the corner tap, boiled them for bathing and tea, and kept going. At first, I complained. Then I felt something unexpected. Pride. I was learning how little was needed to live well.

But while discipline was essential for my survival in the village, I still needed an outlet to let loose. Even though it was "forbidden," Johannesburg's nightlife became the perfect escape for this Queens girl. One of the highlights of my time in South Africa was experiencing that nightlife, a carefree, joyful, completely un-Peace Corps-approved burst of pure life that my soul needed.

The Peace Corps policy was that once you were at your assigned site, you must remain there until it was necessary to visit the office for a medical checkup, an emergency, or training. However, being in our twenties and aware of the exciting events unfolding down in Gauteng, we were eager to explore.

Occasionally, I'd arrange to meet up with other volunteers, especially those nearby. We lived miles apart in different corners of Limpopo; my closest friend lived in Bochum, a long drive from my site. We would gather to organize activities midway between our locations and sometimes travel to Johannesburg for a weekend without informing the Peace Corps. During our time in Pretoria for training, we would sometimes visit Joburg, just about 45 minutes away. We'd go, have fun, and then return to Pretoria by public taxi to sleep in our hostel.

I have fond memories of partying and hanging out in Yeoville from the late 1990s through the early 2000s. It was the place to be, and I felt right at home. The neighborhood was lively, reminding me of Harlem and Brooklyn, a blend of cultures and diverse people that created a one-of-a-kind atmosphere. Maybe I was seeing it through rose-colored glasses, but to me, it always felt safe and vibrant.

Our favorite hangout was Tandoor, a reggae club on Rockey Street that always drew a friendly, mixed crowd. I loved going there. Growing up Caribbean in New York, dancehall music was part of me, so walking into the club, the rhythm, the people, and the sounds all felt instantly familiar and warm. The club had an open rooftop, and that's where everyone wanted to be. It was cooler there, with a nice breeze, and it was the spot where people smoked more than just nicotine. A massive crowd always packed the place, and we'd dance for hours under the stars. The vibe was unmatched.

My favorite nights were those hosted by the hottest DJs of the time: Appleseed (now Jahseed) and DJ Admiral. They were legends back then, especially Appleseed, who was part of the famous group Bongo Muffin. I introduced myself and quickly became friends with them, following their gigs like a groupie. Whenever they played, I had to be there. Those were moments of pure, unadulterated freedom. The daily worries of the township felt miles away, and we were just young people, letting loose.

However, during those carefree moments, we never stopped to ask why the Peace Corps was so strict about our movements. Why couldn't we go wherever we wanted? What exactly were they protecting us from? At the time, it felt like unnecessary control.

It didn't take long for me to learn otherwise. The danger was simple and clear: anything could happen, and if no one knew our location, no one could help us. I'm still grateful that most of our adventures ended without incident. However, one event changed us, making us realize how reckless our escapades had been.

We were riding in a kombi, a shared taxi, with some friends when, as fate would have it, the taxi was involved in an accident. My friend, a fellow volunteer, suffered injuries so severe that she eventually lost half her leg. That moment was a brutal shock, a chilling turning point in my life. When you're this far from home, simple mistakes can carry absolute, devastating consequences. That accident made it painfully clear how crucial it was to be precisely where you were supposed to be at all times.

In the weeks that followed, we became more cautious. The late-night excursions faded, and we refocused on our work. It was a hard lesson, but a necessary one: freedom and responsibility could coexist, but we couldn't afford to be that careless again.

That reminder was reinforced when I was involved in two separate accidents. In one, I had permission to travel outside my site, and in the other, I didn't. The first accident happened while one of my best friends, Shel, was visiting from New York. We had planned a road trip along the Garden Route, a scenic drive known for its breathtaking landscapes and vibrant towns. Shel had taken time off from her job to visit me, and we were excited to explore South Africa together. We rented a car from a local agency in Johannesburg and set off early in the morning, the sun rising over the horizon as we headed south.

The drive was exhilarating. We laughed, sang along to the radio, and took turns at the wheel. The road stretched out before us, winding through lush forests and along the coastline. It felt like a perfect escape from the township's daily routine.

As we approached a small bridge, I was at the wheel. The bridge was narrow, barely wide enough for two cars to pass. I saw a truck approaching from the other side and thought I could beat it and make it across before the truck reached the bridge. I sped up, calculating the distance and the time it would take to clear the bridge.

But I misjudged.

As I reached the bridge, the truck had already sped up and was halfway across. I realized too late that I wouldn't make it. I yanked the wheel to the right to avoid a head-on collision. The car skidded, and I felt the impact as we slammed into the guardrail. The force of the crash jerked us forward, but the seatbelts held tight, saving us from serious injury.

Shel and I were shaken but unharmed. We sat in the car for a moment, catching our breath as our hearts pounded. The truck driver didn't stop; he kept going, leaving us to deal with the aftermath. Other vehicles pulled over, and bystanders came to check on us. Luckily, we had no broken bones, only a few bruises.

I called the car rental company, and they sent a tow truck to remove the damaged vehicle. They provided us with a replacement vehicle, and we continued our journey, albeit more cautiously. We reached our destination later that day, but the thrill of the drive had worn off by then.

The second accident occurred later in my service. Another Peace Corps volunteer, also from New York, and I decided to take a weekend trip to visit another volunteer from Chicago in a nearby town. We didn't have a car, and it was too far to bike, so we decided to hitchhike. It seemed like no big deal at the time. Everyone was doing it. It was something we had never done before, though, and it felt like an adventure.

We stood by the side of the road, thumbs out, waiting for a ride. After a while and several cars later, a small red hatchback pulled over. Two men were in the front seat, the latest kwaito booming and vibrating throughout the car. They rolled down the window and asked where we were going. We told them, and they nodded, motioning for us to get in.

We sized them up and thought we could take them on if they tried anything funny. We climbed into the backseat and buckled up out of habit. That was before we noticed the brown paper bags of their beers between their legs. They turned up the music and sped off. The road blurred as we sped along, the wind whipping through the open windows. The men were talking in a language I didn't understand, but their laughter was infectious.

We were driving on a narrow two-lane road when a truck suddenly appeared from the opposite direction. The driver of the hatchback tried to pass a car in front of us, but he miscalculated the distance. The truck was too close, and he had to swerve sharply to avoid a collision. The car veered off the road and into the tall grass on the side.

The next thing I knew, the car was rolling. It flipped two or three times, landing upright in the bush. The impact was jarring, but we were all conscious. We looked at each other, checking for injuries. Fortunately, we were wearing our seatbelts, and no one was seriously hurt. The men in the front seat were also OK, though shaken. The car was wrecked, but we were able to climb out with nothing more than a few scrapes and bruises. We said a prayer and thanked God for our lives.

The sun was setting, so there was no time to waste. We flagged down another ride as soon as we could and continued our journey. The experience left a lasting mental impression, possibly causing physical damage and microtears as well, which I would deal with years later.

My exploratory trips outside the township weren't always that far away. I often took trips nearby to the small town center, Mokopane (then still called Potgietersrus), where I would feel a difference immediately. In 1999, the town was a mix of old and new: wide streets lined with neat shops, supermarkets that mainly served white families, and offices that still carried the atmosphere of the apartheid era. The divisions were clear in who shopped where, who owned the businesses, and who did the labor. Across those racial lines, the welcome was not always friendly.

I remember one afternoon walking into a shop in town. At first, nothing seemed unusual: shelves of bread, tins of sardines, the cold hum of refrigerators. Then I noticed the shopkeeper was following me. He was not following me casually, out of curiosity, or by chance, but tailing me aisle by aisle, no more than a few steps behind. I stopped at the flour, and he stopped at the flour. I moved on to the soap, and he moved to the soap. His eyes never left me.

By the time I reached the register, I was irritated. I turned to the shopkeeper and said, as politely as I could manage, "Can I help you?"

Before he could respond, the cashier looked up with a look of surprise on her face, tilting her head. "Where are you from? That accent..."

"America," I said flatly.

The change was instant. Both of their faces lit up, their bodies relaxed, and their voices overflowed. "America! Oh my goodness, so far away! We love America!" Smiles and small talk followed, as if we'd been friends forever.

And I stood there, disgusted. Just five seconds earlier, I was a Black South African and a suspect, watched and unwelcome. Now, suddenly, I was considered exotic, admired, and "safe." I wanted to tell them I was the same person in both moments, but they wouldn't have heard it.

I still remember the security guards shadowing me through the aisles of Alexander's and Macy's in Green Acres Mall back home. Those afternoon walks after school always ended the same way: a man in a uniform keeping tabs on every move I made. It didn't matter that I was just a broke teenager killing time; my Blackness made me a permanent suspect. It was heartbreaking to see that same routine play out across the ocean, in a country full of Black faces, where the pattern remained identical.

But what was really sad was that, in Africa, my Americanness seemed to shield me in ways my blackness couldn't. It wasn't a compliment; it was humiliating. A passport shouldn't dictate a person's worth any more than their complexion does.

But enough about the near-disasters and racism. I know you're probably wondering if there is any love story in South Africa. That's the other fun part besides partying in Joburg.

I still laugh when I think about the first time I told my mom and my godmother, who is also my aunt, that I was in love and getting engaged. I called home, all giddy, ready to share my big news.

"In love? Getting engaged?" my mom asked, suspicious already. "With who? How?"

"This guy named Al," I said, smiling into the phone.

"What does he do?" she shot back.

That threw me off. Of all the questions in the world, that was the first one she wanted answered. Not, "Is he kind?" Not, "Does he make you happy?" No. Straight to his résumé.

"He's a taxi driver," I said.

There was a pause long enough for me to hear her inhale sharply on the other end of the line.

"A taxi driver? In South Africa?"

"Yes, Mom. In South Africa. Limpopo province. Mahwelereng township," I said, like I was giving her the GPS coordinates and like she cared.

My godmother didn't miss a beat either. "Lord, have mercy," she muttered. "Have you lost your mind? Does he even have a degree? Remember you have two."

I rolled my eyes, even though they couldn't see me. "What is wrong with y'all? I'm in love, not applying for a bank loan."

They didn't find it as funny as I did.

Looking back, I understand why they panicked. Maybe I was a bit reckless and impulsive. But at the time, it didn't seem reckless at all.

My host mother was friends with Al and worked as a teacher at a school near his house. Now, the more I think about it, I realize she actually set us up. I vividly recall the first time I met him: he visited our house because of his connection to the family. Somehow, evenings that started with the whole family sitting around the TV in oversized pink comfy couches watching the popular soapie, *Generations*, ended with just the two of us. We'd hang out in front of the house, where his taxi was parked, and talk for what seemed like hours.

Al was charismatic, confident, and protective. Although not wealthy, he consistently showed that he cared. I admired his strong work ethic: he was both a caretaker and the breadwinner, always doing his best for his loved ones. He was humorous, friendly, caring, and his lively energy was infectious. With a good physique and a love for playing football, he embodied everything I suddenly desired.

One evening, not too long after we met, as I walked him out to the taxi so he could go home, he turned to me and said, "I love you. I want to be with you."

"What? You just met me. We hardly know each other. How can you tell me you love me?" I asked, bewildered.

He laughed and just repeated himself.

I wish I had understood then how loosely the phrase "I love you" was sometimes used in South Africa. It could mean "I like you" or "I want to be with you" because there was no word that exactly translates to "like" in the local language.

Despite that, I soon found myself falling deeply in love with him. I was head over heels. We started dating, and our connection grew stronger every day.

After a while, I realized I needed a new living arrangement. Trying to keep a relationship going while living with a host family is like trying to keep a secret in a glass house. I needed my own space, somewhere Al could visit without a dozen eyes keeping tabs on us.

I eventually moved into a back room in the house of a local teacher. This was my third home since arriving in South Africa and it turned out to be the one where I'd stay for the rest of my assignment. It was a modest cinder-block space with a cement floor, but it held everything I needed. Calling it a room was generous because it wouldn't have even fit a queen-sized bed. To me, though, it was a palace of privacy.

I had to treat the space like a giant puzzle. Along one wall, I tucked in a narrow twin bed with a floor mat made of recycled plastic bags in front of it. I even hung a purple sarong over the mosquito net that draped the window to make it feel like home. On the other side, I had a two-burner gas hot plate balanced on an old wooden table beside my neatly stacked pots and groceries. Opposite that was my everything desk. It served as my dining table, my study nook, my office, and a storage unit for my bath bucket and the little basin that snugged right under it.

The bathroom was just one door away, but using it was its own little comedy. It actually had taps and plumbing, which I eventually realized were just there for the aesthetic. Not a single drop of water ever made it through those pipes. Instead, I carried my own in from the outdoor tap, one trip at a time. I would boil water in a kettle, pour it into a bucket, and take a bucket bath one scoop at a time.

That modest little room taught me that the 200-dollar stipend I had worried about before joining the Peace Corps was more than enough. I learned that I could live with very little and still enjoy the small pleasures of life, and, of course, love.

With my privacy finally sorted, our love blossomed. That tiny room became almost a second home for Al. He would come by with his sound system, playing music loud enough for me to hear him approaching. He knew everyone and was super friendly and funny; he'd chat with everyone.

Slowly, our interactions grew more personal, and we found ourselves spending more time together alone. We often visited his house to sit with his family and share meals. We made the most of the little we had, and for a while, it felt like we were in our own world, untouched by anything outside those four walls.

But soon enough, that bubble burst. One day, deep into our courtship, I learned that he already had a child. He hadn't said it explicitly, but it was clear to me that his relationship with his baby mama, Nomusa, was over. He spent all his time with me. There was no way he was seeing someone else.

Then, one day, Nomusa stood furious at my gate, her clothes tight with anger, tears streaking the dust on her cheeks.

She yelled, her finger trembling as she pointed at me, "What are you doing with my man? I have a child! Al is my man!"

I was speechless. I had always thought of "baby mama drama" as something wild that only happened to others. But now, it was right in front of me.

My host mother stepped in like a guard, physically placing herself between us. "You need to leave Jennifer alone!" she ordered. "She has nothing to do with this. Al is the one who came after her!"

Nomusa eventually left, and I confronted Al immediately. He tried to reassure me, claiming he sent money and food and was caring for the child, and there was nothing more to it.

I didn't believe a word of it. We had a heated argument, and right then, I decided to leave him. I had already learned my lesson about entangling myself with the wrong man, and I wasn't about to repeat it with him. I let him go.

A couple of days later, one of his sisters called me in a panic. "Aus Jenny," as she used to call me, "you have to come to the house quickly. Al is very sick, and we just got home from the hospital. He drank rat poison."

Rat poison. *What?* I was so confused.

When I got to his house, he was lying in bed with his mother and siblings by his side. Tears started to roll when he turned around and saw me standing there.

"I thought you were going to leave me, so I didn't think I had anything else to live for," he said.

I felt so bad that I rushed in to give him a big hug and reassured him that I loved him too much to abandon him. And just like that, we were back together.

He then told me that I needed to do something with him urgently the next day. We had to go to a Sangoma, a spiritual healer, to complete his healing. I was kind of taken aback, as I've heard mixed reviews about Sangomas, and they sounded scary. But I agreed to go because he was the love of my life and I supported his beliefs; I wanted him to get better. Plus, it kind of sounded like the Voodoo I was all too familiar with from my childhood.

The next morning, at the crack of dawn, he came to pick me up in his taxi. He looked surprisingly stronger than the almost-dying guy who had drunk poison the previous day.

We crept down some back roads I had never traveled down before, finally pulling up in front of a small two-room house with a wire fence. He squeezed my hand before we got out of the vehicle to reassure me that everything was going to be okay.

We walked to the backyard, where a small mud hut stood. An older man sitting on the floor near the doorway motioned for us to take our shoes off and enter. Inside, an older woman in traditional garb whisked around some incense, which quickly filled the room with smoke. We greeted her in Sepedi. Al said a few more things that I couldn't quite make out, and then she pointed for us to sit on the sisal floor mat.

The mat was adorned by several unfamiliar objects. All around the room, there were small boxes, wooden and beaded objects, candles, and jars filled with mysterious items. And then there were the bones. The infamous bones I had heard about. Human or animal? I had no idea.

Next, the Sangoma handed us some cloudy, yellowish concoction to drink. Al went first, and then I took a sip. It tasted quite earthy. Then the Sangoma began speaking rapidly, and Al would respond from time to time. She picked up the bones, put them in a sachet, and shook them. Then she threw them down to the ground. After what seemed like forever, she started pointing out how they were strewn and explained to Al what she saw. He reached into his pocket, gave her some cash, and she handed him a few jars of mysterious contents, then sent us on our way.

We continued dating as if nothing had happened, and we never spoke of that incident again. I didn't tell a soul. Looking back now, I have no idea how I missed such a massive, glaring red flag. Even more confusing was the logic of it all: why was I the one drinking the concoction when he was the one who wasn't feeling well? I never even questioned it until this very moment.

But either way, the bones must have fallen in his favor. Our relationship moved fast, and before I knew it, we were engaged.

We didn't do things small. The engagement party was a grand, community-wide celebration. In the township, you don't just have a quiet dinner with a few friends; you open your gates to the world. We set up a massive tent, rented rows of chairs, and prepared to host the entire neighborhood. And they showed up in droves. In all that noise and music, it was easy to forget the strange, quiet bitterness of the drink I'd swallowed just a few months before.

Al's family went all out with the setup, decorating with flowers and balloons everywhere. A DJ with powerful speakers shook the ground. Across the street, women in headscarves and aprons were already stirring large pots of stew and pap over open fires. Kids ran between the tents, sneaking scones from trays before the adults saw.

When it was time for our entrance, we didn't just walk in; we made a grand entry. That's the only way to describe it. One of Al's cousins lent us a shiny silver BMW, and we pulled up to the top of the street like royalty. From there, we got out, and suddenly it turned into a parade. A brass band started playing. Women let out ululations, high-pitched celebratory cries that made the hairs on my arms stand up. To my American ears, it was electric.

And the clothes. Oh, the clothes. Al and I were perfectly matchy from head to toe. I wore a royal-blue two-piece outfit, with a long dress and jacket, decorated with orange and gold Ndebele beadwork stitched across accenting lines. He wore a black suit with a royal-blue shirt, the shirt's orange-and-blue details matching mine. Back home, I would've thought matching outfits were corny. But in Limpopo, it was a statement: we belong to each other now.

We danced down the red dirt road together, with the crowd following behind us. Kids ran beside us, laughing and pointing; neighbors stood at their gates watching. I had marched at graduations before, but never down a township street, hand in hand with a taxi driver I was about to promise myself to, while half the neighborhood cheered us on. This wasn't just a ceremony; it was their way of saying, "You're one of us now."

Under the tent, the setup was formal yet welcoming. Our high table was positioned at the front, decorated with flowers and sparkling wine. The elders, including Al's mother, uncles, and aunts, took their places at a designated table.

The ceremony itself was long. Very long. Two pastors led it, one in Sepedi and the other translating into English for my benefit. There were prayers, speeches, and more prayers. People got up one by one to offer blessings, advice, and sometimes jokes. I smiled so hard my cheeks ached, clapping when everyone else clapped, bowing my head when they prayed.

Then came the exchange of rings. My hands were trembling, but when the rings slipped on, the whole tent exploded in applause. Someone shouted "Amen!" and the crowd joined in.

That night, I felt utterly celebrated, embraced, and loved. I had found my person; my time in South Africa felt complete.

But outside of my romantic escapades, the mission continued. Some of my proudest moments came from the work I did supporting young people outside the school walls. I realized then that my most impactful work wasn't happening in workshops or assemblies; it was happening in the quiet, private moments when a student finally felt safe enough to open up to me.

I vividly remember two young men who approached me. One was a boy named Lucky. His name always struck me as ironic because, by the time I met him, both of his parents had already died, almost certainly from AIDS. He was sixteen or seventeen, small for his age, with thin arms and a smile that came and went quickly. I remember taking Lucky back and forth to government and welfare offices, fighting to get his school fees paid. I sat with him for hours, helping him apply for his scholarship. In the end, he stayed in school and eventually graduated.

Thabo was another young man whose success remains etched in my memory. Like Lucky, he was talented but faced crushing economic challenges at home. Yet through hard work and perseverance, he earned a university scholarship, graduated, and became a chartered accountant. We are still in touch today. He is making a massive difference in his community as a motivational speaker and business leader, and he even received a scholarship from the U.S. Embassy for a leadership program that brought him to the States for a semester.

We met when he was in high school, and to this day, he remembers the words I used to encourage him. Years later, when he got married in South Africa, I was able to attend his wedding, which was very special. During his speech, he gave me a shout-out, saying it was people like me who believed in him that helped him become the man he is today. I was so proud. It was a wonderful moment.

Stories like theirs made me realize the vital work we were doing as Peace Corps volunteers and changing lives one person at a time. These young people needed someone who cares, an advocate, a representative who could help them see possibilities beyond their current harsh realities. I wanted them to know that HIV, loss, poverty, and a system that seemed to overlook them could not stop them from reaching their potential.

And knowing my two-year volunteer stint was ending shortly, I wanted to leave more than just temporary programs; I aimed to leave a lasting piece of inspiration. I needed a way to show they were seen and that their potential outweighed their struggles, without letting silence have the last word. If only I could create something big and permanent enough to publicize what was happening around us. Leaving that behind would make my mission feel complete. As it turned out, I couldn't find anything appropriate to make use of, so I had to build it, literally.

The Peace Corps encouraged us to take on final projects before our two years of service were over. Inspired by other countries I had heard about, I decided to create an HIV/AIDS arts mural to raise awareness of the disease and spread prevention messages to a wider audience, young and old.

I started by scouting for a location with a large, highly visible wall in the township. Unfortunately, there weren't any such public walls readily available along the main roads. Then I had the idea of seeing whether anyone would be willing to build a wall specifically for this health education purpose. I identified the perfect location right in front of the local police station on the main road at the start of the township.

I began by meeting with my health worker counterparts to gain their buy-in and collaborate on the project. They were supportive and eager to help. Next, I reached out to my NGO counterparts to identify local artists with whom we could collaborate. They suggested a few young men from the community who were talented and enthusiastic.

The hardest part was convincing the police station commander that the wall would be a good addition to their grounds. At the time, the station stood behind a thin wire fence, with a dusty sidewalk in front. It took several meetings with health workers and police officials, but they finally agreed, much to my relief.

We formed a committee, which I chaired, comprising representatives from the Department of Health, the Police, local artists, and the Mayor's office. Funding was a significant challenge. Building a new wall was not included in any department's current budget, and it was not a trivial cost. I put on my fundraising hat, beat the pavement, and raised enough funds from various sources, including the Peace Corps' small grants fund. I also wrote a compelling proposal, pitched it to the managers, and secured a very generous in-kind donation of building materials, including bricks and cement, from a local building company called Midway Bricks.

After several months of planning and designing the mural, which required committee approval, we began building the wall with the help of community members, including parents from the schools I worked at, who volunteered their time. The process was very challenging, and we encountered numerous hurdles, from sudden heavy rains that washed away freshly laid concrete to delays in organizing the volunteer builders. I was watching the construction drag on, realizing I would leave before the painting even began.

The project was so important to me that I requested an additional three months of service in South Africa to see it through to completion. Fortunately, the Peace Corps office approved my request, and I was able to stay and complete the project.

We held a huge official unveiling event with the Mayor as the guest of honor. A marching band from one of the schools led a parade through town, and the community came together to celebrate. The wall and the mural, though a bit faded, still stand to this day.

This project is one of my proudest achievements from my time in the Peace Corps. I knew that by creating this mural, I was contributing to a long-term strategy of breaking the silence around HIV and AIDS in the community.

As I prepared to leave South Africa, I carried more than just the experience of a volunteer. I didn't just pack my bags and leave South Africa with a volunteer certificate. I left as a woman who had fought for children and built a wall to break a silence. The rhythm of Limpopo had fundamentally changed me, and with it came a quiet certainty that I was ready to begin a family of my own.

The HIV mural we completed in Mahwelereng just before I finished my service.

Giving thanks to the community during my official farewell event with the schools.

A special occasion at church with Thabo during my time in South Africa.

Catching up with my younger host sister, Phemelo, in South Africa.

Reuniting with Thabo M. and Thabo T. during a visit back to South Africa.

Chapter Seven

LIVES APART

I winked at the mirror. "You made it, girl."

The badge tapped the glass: JENNIFER ERIE. Regional Program Manager. Africare. The lanyard swung like a pendulum, steady as the hum of the air vent above. I was finally, undeniably hired. The Peace Corps worked its magic, just as all the professionals had told me it would during our informational interviews. My seasons of rejection, at least as it relates to work, were over.

If someone had told me back then that this would be my light at the end of the tunnel, I would never have believed them. Yet somehow, here I was, standing in an Africare restroom, wearing an Africare badge.

Africare was an NGO founded by C. Payne Lucas and Joe Kennedy, African Americans who played a key role in launching the Peace Corps in its early days. Because of that legacy, the organization embodied a spirit akin to the Peace Corps. The pay was modest, barely better than the Peace Corps stipend, and we often joked that it was just Peace Corps, part two. Yet, the mission, the leadership, and the pride of working in one of the few African American-founded international development organizations were priceless.

Just as my Peace Corps service in South Africa was coming to a close, a fellow volunteer, CD Glin, introduced me to a friend of his at this NGO in Washington, D.C. It was Africare. "Tell them I sent you," he said. I did. I reached out before I even left South Africa, and by the time I returned to the U.S., I had an interview waiting.

Receiving the job offer felt like a homecoming; I knew Africare would not only understand my Peace Corps service but truly value it. My first role was Regional Program Manager for Southern Africa, reporting to Kevin Lowther, another early Peace Corps staffer. I supported him as his right hand, managing projects across the region, including Tanzania, Zimbabwe, Malawi, Zambia, and South Africa. The work involved agriculture, refugee resettlement, health, and democracy initiatives. It was an intense role, but it felt like a natural extension of my time in the field, a commitment that the organization's founder, Mr. Lucas, understood perfectly.

Around the time I started at Africare, the 9/11 attacks hit. When the news reached the office that planes had struck the World Trade Center, everyone panicked. I panicked, too. I had family in New York, including my cousin Stephanie. She was more like a little sister to me, and knowing she worked right in the middle of Manhattan made it worse. I sat there worried, my mind racing through every 'what if.'

Fortunately, management let everyone go home for the rest of the day. Since they shut down all public transportation as a preventive measure, I had to walk. I made my way through the strangely quiet streets back to my place in Southwest D.C. by the waterfront. It was a long, heavy walk, but it was the only way to get home.

When I got to my apartment, I looked out the patio window and saw a huge cloud of black smoke rising from across the river. I turned on the TV and watched, stunned, as the news feed showed the Pentagon in flames.

I could see the aftermath from my window. It really hit home how close I had been to being taken out by the attack.

I dialed and redialed my family in New York, but all I got was the mocking hum of a jammed signal. I couldn't get through. I felt so anxious waiting for confirmation that everyone was okay. Finally, the lines cleared, and I heard back from them. Everyone I cared about was relatively safe, and that was a huge relief.

Around that same time, I was still working to bring Al to the U.S. Remember Al, my taxi driver fiancé from South Africa? Painful disasters have a way of making you want to reconnect with the people who matter most. Having him with me became my top priority.

The funny thing is, I remember my interview with Mr. Lucas himself. He had the presence of a grandfather. May he continue to rest in peace, since he passed away a while back. He was warm, yet direct, and not easily impressed. We openly discussed my experiences, and I even proudly told him about my South African fiancé, who was soon to join me. I still remember the incredulous look he gave me.

"You went to Africa. You fell in love. Now you want to bring this man back here?" he asked.

I nodded.

Mr. Lucas shook his head. "You sure you want to marry your field experience. Couldn't you bring back any other souvenir? A drum? A carving? Not a whole husband? Are you sure about this?"

I chuckled and promised to think about it, already mentally dismissing his advice as I headed for the door.

What Mr. Lucas didn't know was that the so-called souvenir had already been bubble-wrapped in paperwork. Two weeks before leaving Pretoria, I mailed the K1 visa application to the State Department. In my tote bag sat a plastic folder labeled FUTURE MBOYANE FAMILY PACK, filled with love letters, bus tickets, pictures, and a wrinkled engagement-ring receipt as proof that I was, in fact, in love with my field experience and that this was not a scam, not a fling, not a green card plot. This bond was forever.

"Field Experience" himself was rolling up his finest clothes and shoes, cramming them into a faux-leather suitcase, and practicing the line he'd use at the Embassy visa section: I'm going to join my future wife.

Soon, my Al was on his way. I took care of everything, from visa fees and the plane ticket to paperwork, and even sent him some money for new clothes. At work, advice came whether I wanted it or not. Some shared stories of women who'd done the same and later regretted it, and warnings about the risks if anything happened to him while he was far from home.

Even my family did not cut me any slack. I remember my sister organizing an intervention, a last attempt to show me some sense, as my mother put it. They gathered: my mother, Nancy, and my godmother.

Nancy went first: "If he loves you, let him make his own sacrifice. Let him find his way here."

"He can't," I shot back. "He doesn't have that kind of money."

"Doesn't he own a taxi?" my godmother asked, always the practical one.

"It's not his taxi," I said, maybe sharper than I intended. "He drives someone else's."

That was the truth: he was the firstborn of a fatherless family, and their sole breadwinner. Whatever he earned went to them. There was nothing left to save. That was why I had to do it.

My mother leaned in, her tone steady but sharp enough to cut.

"Petit mwen, *my child*, you're rushing into this. This path is not your destiny. Wap kon Joj," she quipped in Creole, which means something like "just wait and see what will happen to you" and not in a positive way.

When my mother spoke, I could feel her words laced with a warning carved from a lifetime of surviving betrayal. Her words came from her own story: a young Haitian woman who fell in love in America, only to watch the man she chose vanish into another woman's life. In her voice, I heard the echo of that old sorrow and the fear that I might repeat the same pattern she had spent decades avoiding.

96

Nancy didn't waste time either. She went straight for the old wound. "Why do you always go for misfits? Remember that boyfriend who ended up in jail?"

That memory was a raw slap in the face. It was the one bit of history I wished no one else remembered, and now Nancy had thrown it onto the table.

I met Nancy's gaze, my eyes asking, "Are you serious right now?" before I quickly swallowed the tears rising in my throat.

Misfits? Was that what they thought? Was I collecting broken men like souvenirs? I kept quiet and let them talk themselves out. They could have their word, but I knew deep down that I would still have my way.

"Al is not like that. He's different. He's responsible. You'll see."

Al was not some shadow from my past. He was hardworking and well-respected in Mahwelereng. He wanted me, and I wanted him. He was mine. And besides, if something was hard to get, that was exactly what I wanted. They simply didn't know Al. I was sure that once they met him, they would see things differently.

So, when the day arrived, I was at the airport, confidently standing in my new heels, ready to pick up my so-called souvenir and start a life with my man.

The first few weeks went fast. We were busy settling in and introducing Al around, and soon we had a routine. I went to my job at Africare, and Al took on the task of learning Washington, D.C., and figuring out what kind of job he could get. He quickly made a few friends through my friends, i.e., their husbands and partners. I was happy when he eventually found a South African diaspora crowd. I loved watching him charm everyone, including my skeptical mother. I saw it as a sign of his easy-going, sensitive nature. We hosted small dinners or went out to eat with friends, and for a short, beautiful time, we were on cloud nine.

Not long after Al arrived, we planned our wedding and finalized the immigration paperwork. We didn't have a big "white" wedding, as they call it in South Africa; instead, we had a small civil ceremony with the justice of the peace, followed by a small reception at my sister's house in Maryland. My mother and my cautious godmother were there, along with a few other friends and family, including Mr. Lucas and Kevin from the office. Everyone was happy. It worked out. Didn't I tell them? I was now proudly Mrs. Jennifer Mboyane. Somebody's *whole* wife.

But even in hindsight, I realize Al was struggling to adjust. It was not easy for him to find a job. He had no formal qualifications and wanted a job that paid better than driving a taxi back home. So, I paid for his Commercial Driver's License course. He put in the effort, passed the test, and landed a job with a contractor trucking in the Washington, D.C., area. His new pay was nothing compared to what I brought home, so even with him driving a big truck, I was still the primary breadwinner.

I quickly learned that Al was a traditional, patriarchal man who believed the husband provided and the wife stayed home. But America messed with that hierarchy and flipped it upside down. Suddenly, he was stuck in a low-paying job while I climbed the career ladder, and in turn, he became incredibly insecure.

Suddenly, I had to explain every phone call and every minute I was late coming home. If I talked about work, Al saw it as a threat to our life together. I constantly had to reassure him I wouldn't leave him for an "accomplished man" from the office. At first, I thought his possessiveness was sweet and flattering, but it soon became unsettling.

He viewed everything through a lens of disrespect. If I suggested we save money or asked him to help with chores, he claimed I thought I was "better than him" because I earned more. We were on two completely different wavelengths. His logic was so disconnected from reality that I began to wonder if this was more than just a cultural adjustment.

In the midst of all that, I found out I was pregnant with our son, Anthony Kagiso. I had hoped the marriage and the coming baby would anchor us both, but things only seemed to deteriorate further. Even after Anthony was born, the trouble didn't ease; in fact, it deepened.

I owe so much to my mother during that time. She had never really talked to me about pregnancy or babies, but the moment Anthony was born, she dropped everything. She came running for her first grandchild and stepped in as his full-time nanny. She delighted in every little thing he did, and her support was the lifeline I didn't even know I needed.

Mom even accompanied me to Anthony's doctor visits when Al couldn't get off work. During one visit, the pediatrician diagnosed Anthony with asthma and asked if anyone in the house smoked. I looked straight at her. The doctor explained that even secondhand smoke could ruin his health. Right then and there, my mother decided to quit. She went cold turkey and never picked up a cigarette again. It was a massive sacrifice, but she did it purely out of love for her grandson.

Anthony was a lovely baby, sweet, calm, and easy. He was never the wild, dirt-digging, frog-chasing kind of boy. He was quiet, observant, thoughtful, and very obedient even as a child. He hardly cried, and I used to joke that he got his laid-back nature from me.

But then I noticed Anthony wasn't babbling much, even around ten to twelve months. The books said he should be saying "mama" or "dada" by then, but he was quiet. I mentioned it to his pediatrician, who suggested we take him for testing, and lo and behold, he was diagnosed with a speech delay.

Early on, we started occupational therapy at the children's hospital. In preschool, Anthony joined special programs to build his skills. Eventually, he was diagnosed with ADD. I specify the diagnosis without the "H" because he wasn't hyperactive at all; he remained a joy to everyone.

I wish I could say the same about his father. Things with Al deteriorated fast. His behavior became suffocating. His paranoia grew, and the emotional abuse intensified. I began to worry his temper might turn physical. Thank goodness it never reached that level.

One night, after putting Anthony to sleep, I sat on my bed catching up with my friend Claudia, who also worked at Africare, on the phone. It was just harmless chatter about motherhood and work. When I hung up and walked toward the kitchen, I jumped. Al stood in the doorway, arms crossed, menacing, with bloodshot eyes.

He didn't speak at first. He just stared. Then, out of nowhere, he snapped, "So… who are you meeting on Friday?"

I blinked. "What?"

"Don't act like I didn't hear you. You said something about Friday. I'm not stupid."

I tried to laugh it off. "We were talking about a school event. You really think I'm—"

He cut me off, waving his hand like he was brushing away flies. "Ah, you American women think you're slick. Always got something lined up." He paced the floor, his voice rising and falling like a radio with weak reception. "You think I don't hear you? You said you have doubts. Doubts about me?"

He stopped and glared. "When I ask, it's always 'nothing.' Always work or a friend. You think I'm dumb because I drove a taxi? You're speaking in code now."

My heart pounded. I stood there speechless.

He let out a dry, bitter laugh. "You see? You can't even answer. That's how guilty people look. You smile too much on the phone. You say 'oh really?' like you're talking to a man. I know that tone. That's the tone women use when they are *flirtious*."

Flirting, I thought, correcting him in my head.

"Al, that's crazy," I said. "You're making up stories. I was talking to Claudia as usual. You know her husband."

He shook his head slowly. "Crazy? No. You'll see. When the truth comes out, when you're standing there with your papers and your smart English, you'll remember this. The color of the cow grows on the calf."

I blinked, trying to decode the metaphor. Where did cows come into this?

He walked away, mumbling about "people pretending" and how everyone changes once they get a job title. I stood there holding the phone, stunned.

"Al," I said, "this isn't love. I can't live like this."

He turned back, his voice and hands trembling. "If you leave me, I'll die."

I remembered South Africa and the rat poison incident. I wasn't going to let that happen again. I went to him, hugged him, and suggested counseling. "Maybe we need help. We need a professional to help us strengthen our marriage."

The room went still. The baby monitor hummed in the background. For a moment, I hoped for a human response. Instead, he shook his head and muttered about women who think they are wiser than men.

After months of convincing, he finally agreed to go. He protested all the way, saying Africans fix their own homes. I found a practice with a Nigerian male counselor and an African American woman, hoping he would feel seen. He sat on the far edge of the couch, stiff and guarded.

After a few sessions, he quit. He accused the counselors of being on my side and trying to convince me to leave him.

I finally reached my breaking point.

"If you don't continue, our relationship is over," I told him.

It was a direct ultimatum. I wasn't sure if he took me seriously, so I contacted a lawyer and started the paperwork immediately.

First came the physical separation. I moved out and got my own place in Maryland. Since the lease was in my name, I told him he had to leave, too. He found his own place, and we grew further apart. Maryland law required a two-year separation before a final divorce, so we waited. Things never improved. He made no effort to reconcile.

The court proceedings were as messy as the marriage itself. Al insisted on representing himself and refused an attorney. It was a disaster. It pained me, but I asked for sole physical and legal custody of Anthony. I knew shared custody would just mean more drama and constant battles for approval. By the grace of God, the judge granted me 100% custody. If Al had used a lawyer, he probably would have received a fifty-fifty split.

The court ordered child support to be garnished directly from his paycheck and granted him visitation rights. At first, he came every other weekend. Then he started showing up late, and finally, he stopped coming altogether. I would get Anthony dressed and excited, only to have to make excuses for his father and find something else to distract him when Al stood him up.

A few months later, the money stopped too. I realized Al had stopped working altogether and dropped out of the system. Years later, after we had already started living overseas, I found out through a mutual friend that Al eventually became unhoused. Worried, I coordinated with him and another friend's husband to try to find him, but after a while Al disappeared on them too, and we lost the trail. I later asked one of my friends for the number of a private investigator so I could pass it along to his family, hoping they might be able to reach him and help him return to Limpopo, where at least he would have their support. As far as I know, he might still be out on the streets of the D.C. metro area today, and it makes me sad.

As we know, life doesn't stop for anyone; it just keeps moving. I often wished for the luxury to stay home, exhale, and actually process the pain of my marriage crumbling so fast, but I never got that chance. Life simply pushed me forward.

I found myself balancing four parallel stories. There was the "souvenir" love I had brought all the way from South Africa, now lost. There was my beautiful baby boy, who remains my greatest blessing to this day. There was my mother, stepping up when I needed her most. And finally, there was the job I had always dreamed of. At least three of those four stories were still holding firm.

When Anthony turned four, a pattern I did not want to see

started to come into focus. I stood in the kitchen lighting his birthday candle, watching the flame sputter out twice before it finally held on the third try. The little number four glowed like a reminder I was trying to outrun. That was the age my father left and never returned, and now my son was four, with his father gone too. His absence felt like a scar Anthony was bound to inherit, as if loss itself were being passed down. It did not feel random; it felt like a cruel repetition, like life had traced the same line twice and decided to call it fate. I wanted to believe I'd broken the cycle, but under the light of that stubborn candle, I realized the cycle was still spinning. Right then, I vowed to be the one to stop it.

But fate, I realized, only writes the first few lines. The rest is about who shows up, and this time, that included me. I didn't wait for destiny to change the script; I fought back with choice. I got out of bed every morning, went to work, and created the home my son deserved.

Thankfully, I wasn't alone in that fight. My mother was there, holding the line. I never had to send Anthony to daycare with strangers. She cared for him from the beginning.

This woman held the fabric of three generations together without ever asking for credit or sympathy. I didn't see it back then, but I see it now. She didn't teach me how to be a perfect mother, but she taught me what endurance looks like and how to be always there. This time, when the pattern tried to repeat, I could stand on my own because she was supporting us. My son still had a home, a mother, an aunt, and a grandmother who showed up and loved him unconditionally. My mother had always been our rock.

I made a vow then to succeed, not just for my career, but to build a stable life that could hold all of us together.

Bono, the lead singer of U2, during his visit to Africare House in Washington, D.C.

Meeting with Mr. Lucas and President Museveni during my time with Africare.

Chapter Eight

STEPPING INTO DIPLOMACY

That vow became my compass. It pushed me into rooms I didn't feel ready for and decisions I didn't yet know how to carry. Around that time, I heard from another friend, Jabu, Anthony's godfather, who had also served as a Peace Corps volunteer in South Africa.

"Hey, Jen," he said. "Someone I know at John Snow Incorporated (JSI) is looking for a Program Coordinator. It's in public health, logistics, and supply chain. Interested?"

I had never worked in supply chain, but the role was described as more managerial and administrative, with the expectation that I would learn logistics on the job. The salary was significantly higher than what I was earning at Africare, making the offer immediately attractive.

I interviewed, and I got the job. But honestly? Walking away from Africare was not easy. I was so appreciative that they took a chance on me and gave me my first real development job. Also, I loved working for icons like Mr. Lucas and Kevin, and was very proud of the work we did as the premier African American non-governmental organization working in Africa. I will always cherish the unprecedented access I had, being surrounded by people who looked like me, all pouring our hearts into the betterment of the motherland. It's not every day you get that kind of access to presidents and celebrities, like Museveni and Bono, while doing work that actually matters.

Luckily, JSI turned out to be a fantastic environment. I found the Peace Corps network was also strong there. While the office was predominantly white, unlike at Africare, everyone was lovely. I remember the director of our project used to rollerblade to work from faraway Bethesda, Maryland, all the way to Rosslyn, Virginia. I'd bump into him in the lobby, in spandex shorts and a tank top, sweating profusely, clearly a director who didn't take himself too seriously.

I spent six incredible years at JSI, and looking back, it was a whirlwind. I started out on the Deliver Project, cutting my teeth on reproductive health and family planning in Tanzania and Zimbabwe. But the real game-changer came when I helped pull together a winning proposal for the Supply Chain Management Systems (SCMS) project.

This wasn't just another project. It became the largest HIV/AIDS commodities effort USAID had ever funded, with a budget that literally ran into the billions. Being part of the founding team felt like being at the center of the world. Before I knew it, I was promoted to Country Program Manager, supervising directors across Nigeria, Zimbabwe, and South Africa. I loved the weight of that responsibility. The global scope of it all finally matched the size of my ambitions.

The best part, though, was the people. My supervisors, Marilyn, Rich Ainsworth (RIP), and Greg, weren't just bosses; they were truly fantastic human beings. Between my amazing office mates and the Friday afternoon happy hours, JSI became one of the best places I've ever worked. We worked hard, but we actually liked each other and had lots of fun together.

But as my career took flight, my heart started to tug in another direction. The job required me to be a frequent flyer, constantly bouncing between D.C. and our country programs. Every time I packed a suitcase, I felt the sting of leaving Anthony behind with my mom. I hated the distance. Those short-term trips were starting to feel longer and longer, and I realized my priorities were shifting. I didn't just want a big career anymore; I needed a role that didn't force me to choose between the world and my son. I wanted a way to take my whole world with me.

That's when I began seriously considering government roles, including at the State Department, but especially with USAID. It felt like the perfect mix: meaningful international work, the opportunity to live abroad, and the security of housing, schooling, and family allowances. For a single mother eager to see the world, it seemed ideal.

Maybe it was practical. Maybe it was a little bit of escapism. Probably both. Travel had always helped me heal; moving gave me comfort, and distance provided perspective. In some ways, leaving felt like the only way to stay whole. This inner conflict made my decision to pursue a career in government feel both necessary and deeply personal.

But beneath my desire to travel was a deeper need for stability. I was tired of moving from one project to the next, never sure if the next grant would come through or if I'd have to start over. While development work was exciting, it often felt like being with someone passionate but also somewhat unpredictable.

I used to joke that federal jobs were like ironclad relationships: difficult to get into and even harder to get out of. Someone once told me, "They never fire government employees; they just promote the slow ones sideways." It made me laugh. Secretly, I loved the sound of it. I wanted a job that wouldn't be lost every few years. I wanted something stable, something Anthony could grow up around without constant upheaval.

So my mission became to find stability for us. One night, I told my mother, "If I ever get a post abroad, I'm taking you and Anthony with me." She looked over her glasses, putting her word-find puzzle book to the side, half proud, half skeptical, her mouth twitching. "We'll see, child," she said. "We'll see."

Maybe it was hope, or just a deep instinct to keep moving until everything felt stable again. Either way, this mindset led me to apply for government jobs. Whatever the reason, filling out those application forms was my first step toward rewriting my story.

People often say that when you're ready to learn, the right teacher shows up. That's exactly what happened to me.

It was February, and at JSI I was co-hosting a Black History Month talk with an older colleague, Vance Shaw. I remember walking into the conference room that day with my notebook in hand and sitting in the front row, more out of curiosity than anything else. The speaker was a U.S. Ambassador, a rotund, charismatic Black man with the calm authority that only comes from decades of navigating politics and people. His name was Harry Thomas, Jr., and he was a good friend of Vance's.

He started sharing his story, and somewhere between anecdotes about postings and policy, he mentioned that he was from Queens, New York.

I almost screamed. Queens! My Queens. I was very pleasantly surprised.

After his talk, I waited to avoid being the first to rush him, but stayed close enough to make sure he didn't leave before I said something.

When I finally got to him, I said, "Thank you for your inspirational talk. You said you're from Queens?"

He smiled. "Yes, I did. Hollis, Queens, to be exact."

"No way," I said in shock. "I went to school in Hollis."

His eyes lit up. "Which one?"

When I told him it was Linden Junior High School, he nodded. "Oh, I know that school. Good school."

We kept talking, and I told him I wanted to work for the U.S. government and be like him when I grew up. Unlike most people, he listened and invited me to visit his office the very next week. He was the Chief of Staff for the entire U.S. Foreign Service at the State Department. Normally, I wouldn't have gotten past the front desk. What were the odds???

When I got to his office in Foggy Bottom, I sat across from him with my folder of papers, feeling like a stack of unfinished homework. He scanned my résumé, listened to my story, and then looked up.

"You could join the State Department," he said, "but honestly? You'd be bored."

I was surprised, but he just smiled.

"You seem like someone who wants to be where things are happening and get your hands dirty."

"Bored?" I asked. "You're a diplomat, how could that be boring?"

He smiled and said, "We spend our time in meetings and writing cable reports to Washington. I can tell from your experience that you like being out in the field, working directly with people. Trust me, you should be at USAID."

I told him I'd dreamed of becoming an ambassador one day, like him.

He said, "Well, some USAID officers *do* become ambassadors. It's not impossible." He paused for a beat before adding, "In fact, I think I know someone you should meet."

I think I floated out of that office.

The Ambassador was a man who didn't waste time. Within days, I met with his friend, Alonzo Fulgham, the Acting Administrator of USAID. Of all people, the head of the very agency that he says I should work at. Again, what are the odds? The speed of the connection alone was astonishing, but when I walked into Alonzo's office, I was in for another surprise. He was another impressive leader, warm, encouraging, and a Black man at the top of his field. I was amazed. In the same week, two very accomplished Black men offered me mentorship. It felt like everything was coming together. This was my moment.

He welcomed me warmly. "So, I hear you want to join USAID? Is that so?"

"Yes," I said. "Very much."

He smiled, almost fatherly. "Good. Don't worry about what I can or can't do. Just apply. When you see a position that fits, send me a note. We'll see what happens from there." He then asked me if I knew someone named Art Brown, and I told him no. He gave me Art's contact info and told me to talk to him before I submitted my application. Little did I know at that time that Art was like the Godfather for all Black people trying to break into USAID.

I followed Alonzo's advice. I visited the USAJobs website, which felt like a maze designed to discourage applicants, and began browsing the labyrinth of listings. I didn't settle for the first decent title I saw. I kept searching until I found "Health Officer" at USAID. When I saw the posting, I hesitated. The logical side of me reminded me of the thousands who apply and the slim chance of success, but my gut feeling was stronger. My entire career, from the Peace Corps to Africare to JSI, felt like one long introduction leading to this moment. I had to try. I also reached out to Art, who immediately accepted my request for a phone call. I don't remember which country he was posted in at the time, but he had already been with the agency long enough to know all the ins and outs and provided me with invaluable advice on how to fill out the application.

I submitted my application just before midnight, heart racing with excitement. Then everything went quiet. Weeks passed with no news, and I began to doubt I'd made it. I spoke to colleagues at JSI about it, and they were all super supportive, including my supervisor.

Then one morning, I saw an email: "USAID: You've been shortlisted for an interview." I stared at the screen, struggling to believe it was real.

I spent the next few days devouring every textbook,

newspaper, and policy paper I could find. I wasn't going to let this chance slip away because of a technicality. The interview process was grueling. It was an all-day event, the kind that tests not just your experience but also your endurance. There was a timed written exercise in the morning on a computer, a panel interview with four poker-faced officers, and a group activity alongside 3 other candidates where everyone silently competed.

By the afternoon, I was running on fumes and honestly almost gave up on making it through the final panel. I was trying to ignore the exhaustion, focusing only on the questions, when one of the Health Officers looked down at my résumé. Her name was Carol Carpenter Yaman, a USAID legend.

She paused. "You know Richard Ainsworth?" she asked, looking up.

My heart skipped. "Yes," I said carefully. "He's my current supervisor at JSI."

Her expression softened into the faintest smile. "I used to work with Rich in Cairo, back in the late 1990s. He's a brilliant man."

That small exchange lasted only a few seconds, but it changed the atmosphere in the room. Suddenly, I wasn't just another candidate; I was someone connected to a person she respected. I realized then how relationships can travel farther than we do. Sometimes your name walks into a room long before you do, and if you've treated people well, that name opens the door a little wider.

A few weeks later, I got the call.

"Congratulations. We're pleased to inform you that you've been selected for the position of Health Officer with USAID."

I had to ask her to repeat it twice, just to be sure.

I sat at my desk for a long time, staring at the computer screen, feeling the weight of years: the Peace Corps, the late nights, the tears, the hopes. All of it converged into that one moment. It wasn't just luck. It was timing, grace, and readiness meeting an opportunity. Blessings all around, crowning a commitment that spanned over 10 years.

I thought of Ambassador Thomas and Alonzo, whose belief had opened the door, and of Richard, whose reputation had quietly pushed me through, and of Art, who guided me through the last mile. Maybe the Ambassador had pulled a string, but I preferred to believe it was a mix of grace, readiness, and a lot of divine intervention. Because when the student is ready, the teacher appears. And sometimes, that teacher wears a State Department badge and changes the entire course of your life.

When I finally found my voice, I dialed my mother.

"Mom," I said, the words thick with relief. "We did it. We're going to work for the U.S. government."

She laughed. "We?"

"Yes, we." Then I called Nancy next and gave her the good news.

I was so excited, even though I had no idea what was coming next. I hoped for an assignment in Africa, but honestly, I was just happy to finally join the professional world I had worked so hard to reach. It felt like I was stepping into something lasting. I kept reminding myself that this was the U.S. government, a federal agency. The highest level of our government. Agencies like this don't merely just exist; they create legacies. I had made it into an institution that would be my forever home until I chose to retire.

I later learned that USAID receives over twenty thousand applicants for some Foreign Service jobs. Even if it were only half that, it still seemed wild. So yes, I felt thrilled, proud, and a little scared all at once. As an implementing partner, my work at Africare and JSI gave me visibility into how USAID works, since we were funded by them. The rhythm of development work was already woven into everything I did.

When you join as a Foreign Service Officer, you don't find out your assignment right away. First, you go to Washington, D.C. for training, and only after that do you learn where you'll be posted. The wait added suspense; it was exciting, but also the first real administrative stress test.

The onboarding program lasted about six weeks. There were forty of us in my group, 10 of whom were Health Officers, a mix of eager newcomers and experienced development professionals. I met my New York "twin" in our cohort named Ruth, from Long Island, who is one of the smartest and sweetest people I've ever met. During those weeks, we got a crash course in what it means to represent the United States abroad: the policies, the politics, and the endless paperwork required to navigate it all.

One big challenge was the foreign language requirement. We had to be fluent in a language other than English, but there was a proficiency test available to skip the months-long language training. I remember looking through the list and spotting Haitian Creole. Wait a second. I can actually do that one. I had picked it up over the years at home and felt comfortable speaking it. I knew that bypassing the training would let me escape the long D.C. wait, so I decided to just go for it, even if it didn't automatically mean I would be posted to Haiti.

I signed up for the test, practiced with my mom, and to my great relief, I passed on the first go. One box checked. That meant I didn't have to stay in D.C. as long as some of my colleagues. I was secretly happy about that because I wanted to leave on the summer cycle. With Anthony, timing mattered. I wanted to get to my new post before the school year started so he could settle into an international school without disruption.

The language test was the last thing I could actively control; the rest of my future and Anthony's schedule were now sealed within the folders stacked on the assignment board's table. Six weeks of intense training had brought me here: the official Flag Day Ceremony. Standing on the brink of this moment I had envisioned so many times, my hands trembled in a way I couldn't ignore. This wasn't just my career; it was the milestone every new Foreign Service Officer would remember for the rest of their lives.

The ceremony was held in a big conference room with polished floors and high ceilings. Forty of us sat there with our family and friends, dressed in our best suits, waiting to hear which country would define the next two years of our lives. It felt like both a graduation and a judgment.

I came with my mother, my sister Nancy, and my son Anthony, my quiet, intuitive, wide-eyed little boy who was almost seven and full of questions. A couple of colleagues from JSI also came to cheer me on, including Carrie and Naomi, with whom I'm still close to this day. I wore a fitted black skirt suit, blue shirt, and heels, determined to present myself as if I already belonged among the ambassadors.

However, the formality didn't diminish our fun family spirit. We huddled together, playing a game and whispering guesses about the countries still remaining on the board.

When the ceremony started, each name was announced one at a time. The flags disappeared in alphabetical order, and I kept running through the list of African countries in my head.

"Still plenty left," I muttered. "Namibia, Niger, Nigeria, Rwanda, Senegal, Tanzania..." When they reached O and Oman was called, I leaned forward. Next was P: Panic, Passport, Perfect. I whispered the African options to myself: "Portugal? No, that's Europe. Papua New Guinea? Nope, that's too far."

Then my name was called.

I stood, smiled, and walked to the front, concealing my many guesses. The floor seemed unsteady, and my heels wobbled, while my heart pounded with anticipation.

The facilitator handed me a small flag and said,

"Congratulations. You're going to the Philippines."

For a moment, I stood still. The Philippines? My mind kept searching: Which 'P' is that? I hadn't even thought of it. I was sure that my years of field work were destined for Africa. Asia was a whole new world. The tiny flag landed in my palm, showing stars, a sun, and no savanna.

I accepted the flag, maintaining a professional demeanor despite my disbelief.

Back in our row, Mom blinked and said, "Your ancestors are

lost." Nancy laughed, and Naomi added, "You're going to Asia, girl."

"Apparently, we are," I said, a wide grin finally breaking the professional smile as I tucked the flag away, a million questions racing across my brain.

Anthony watched us, picking up on the excitement even if he didn't fully understand what had changed. And I knew everything had changed for us. The waiting was over. Having moved from a Peace Corps volunteer to a non-profit field leader, and now finally a USAID Foreign Service Officer, we were no longer just responding to circumstances; we were shaping our own path.

When I received the assignment to the Philippines, it felt both exhilarating and daunting. I spent the next few months in Washington, D.C., researching everything I could about Manila, learning the ropes of how headquarters operated, and getting to know my new colleagues in the Global Health Bureau. It was a crash course in diplomacy, development, and bureaucracy all at once. I was fortunate to be mentored by a great senior director, whose calm guidance and sharp insights helped me navigate the maze of new acronyms, systems, and expectations. Those months at HQ became a grounding period before I packed up my entire life and moved halfway around the world to Manila with my mom, just in time to get Anthony settled and ready to start the new school year.

With my friend Naomi, whom I met at JSI, we've been friends ever since.

With my mentor, Ambassador Harry K. Thomas Jr., in Washington, D.C.

With my JSI supervisor, Richard Ainsworth.

Chapter Nine

EAST OF EVERYTHING FAMILIAR

When the moving crew arrived, I knew my life had shifted gears for good. I was no longer just a New Yorker scraping by; I was becoming part of the U.S. government machinery.

In Queens, moves were gritty neighborhood affairs. Relatives and neighbors showed up late, in whatever clothes they had on, hauling mismatched boxes up five flights of stairs.

This time it was the U.S. government.

A crew of professionals walked in, wearing matching shirts and carrying rolls of white paper and custom crates. They carefully wrapped each plate and picture frame as if they were museum artifacts.

While they handled the "Fine China," I was hunched over rechecking our new diplomatic passports. And then again. I stared at my name until it stopped looking real. I checked my mother's photo. Anthony's. I turned the black covers over in my hands, as if they might suddenly change.

My mother, always busy and energetic, was taking a peaceful moment for herself. She kindly reached for a stack of dishes to assist the packers.

"Mom, stop," I said, catching her arm and laughing. "They do everything. We're not allowed to help."

She froze, hand hovering, staring at the men sealing crates with official tape. Half proud, half skeptical, her mouth twitching the way it did when something felt too good to be true. For a woman who had moved us from basements to apartments through sheer grit and desperation, letting strangers carry the load was almost suspicious.

"Mom, it is okay," I said softly. "You don't have to do a thing."

She turned away, busying herself with her word-find puzzles, but I caught the hitch in her shoulder. She was hiding a tear, or maybe just the shock of finally laying down the weight.

As the packers worked, my mind drifted to Haiti, my mom's home country. It was August 2010, only six months after the 7.0 earthquake had flattened Port-au-Prince and taken more than 200,000 lives. The images still played on loop in my head, rubble, dust-covered faces, entire neighborhoods gone in seconds. It felt personal. What if my parents had never left? What if I'd been born there, grown up there? Would I even have a home to pack right now?

There was a strange irony in my destination, too. I was packing up to move to the Philippines, a region famous for its own volatile tectonic plates. It seemed I was destined for shaky ground.

But I'd already survived my own disaster. People often call a divorce an "earthquake," but mine felt more like a tsunami. Yet, as I watched my belongings disappear into those crates, I realized that the human spirit is built for the aftermath. We are a resilient species; we scavenge through the wreckage, salvage what still works, and rebuild.

A few weeks later, after the movers hauled away every crate and the house echoed empty, we headed to Manila.

I remember the airplane door opening in Manila, and a wave of heat hit me immediately. It was thick and humid, a tropical weight that seemed to test every pore. After twenty-four hours in the air, the longest flight of my life, the sweat started to form the second I stood still. Honestly, I didn't mind. I'll take a hundred degrees over a New York winter any day.

As we walked toward immigration, I looked around the crowded terminal and realized that for the first time, there wasn't a single person who looked like us. This was Asia, and we were truly, visibly the minority.

I gripped Anthony's hand a little tighter. He was wide-eyed, taking everything in, and I found myself leaning down to whisper a quick prayer: *Please, don't say the first thing that comes into your head.* I was waiting for a "Why is everyone..." question that would echo through the hall.

My mother walked on my other side, her small frame fitting squarely into the flow of the crowd around us. She didn't seem to carry a shred of my "foreigner" anxiety; she just adjusted her bag and kept moving with a quiet, unbothered confidence. Seeing her and Anthony there, breathing that same heavy, humid air, my own nerves began to fade. I didn't need to find a home in Manila; I had carried it with me on that extremely long flight. Home was just the three of us, standing in a new city, breathing together.

Once we cleared the humidity of the terminal and stepped outside, the "Diplomatic Treatment" moved up another level. An embassy driver was waiting for us, looking sharp in a pressed white U.S. Embassy polo shirt. He held a sign that read ERIE in bold letters, a sight that made my chest swell just a little.

He greeted us with a broad smile and a rapid-fire stream of Tagalog, which we didn't understand, but it sounded like a warm welcome nonetheless.

"Maligayang pagdating sa Pilipinas! Kumusta po kayo?"

I froze for a second, my brain scrambling for any of the phrases I'd tried to memorize on the plane. I ended up just nodding and giving him a high-wattage "diplomatic" smile that I hoped meant *"thank you,"* not *"I am confused."*

"Yes," I said, a bit too enthusiastically. "Exactly. Thank you!"

Before I could even reach for a strap, he had carefully taken all of our bags. I stood there with my hands empty, watching him load our lives into a clean, air-conditioned vehicle. For a woman who had spent years hauling her own gear through dusty NGO outposts, this felt like a dream. I could get used to this.

My mother sat in the front seat, her gold and diamond-studded earrings shimmering in the afternoon light. Even after twenty-four hours of travel, she looked effortlessly composed, dressed as if she expected to be photographed at any moment. You would have thought she was the diplomat, and I was just along for the ride. While I was staring at the chaos outside, I knew she was already mentally measuring for curtains and scouting a place for the huge soup pot. She had a knack for making the unfamiliar feel like home; it was a quiet magic I'd admired my whole life.

As our embassy driver navigated the gridlock, the van didn't just move through Manila. It fought through it. Outside, the air was a hazy soup of exhaust and humidity, and the streets were a sensory overload of colorful jeepneys, stray dogs, and families living in makeshift stalls right along the road. It was a far cry from the manicured lawns of Maryland.

Above us, the "spaghetti lines", Manila's infamous tangled webs of electrical wires, looped between buildings like overgrown vines. They twisted and knotted in ways that looked both impossible and worrying, a disorganized web hanging over a city that never stopped moving.

In the back, Anthony pressed his face against the window, breathing little clouds onto the glass. Each time it cleared, he leaned in again, caught between wonder and fatigue. His small finger darted toward everything that moved: brightly painted buses, a man balancing a tower of plastic chairs on a motorcycle, and boys playing basketball on cracked pavement.

I watched them too, completely amazed. They were playing a full-speed game, jumping and pivoting with incredible grace, some in tattered flip-flops, but many of them completely barefoot. I had never seen anything like it. In New York, the shoes were the uniform, but here, it was clear that as long as you had feet, you could play.

For a while, Anthony said nothing. He just watched the world blur past, his face tight with a quiet, mounting disbelief. Then, he let out a long, theatrical sigh.

He turned to me, his voice small, worried, and sounding almost like a tiny retiree who had seen too much. "Mom?" he whispered. "People... live here?"

My heart gave a little squeeze. I reached over and took his hand, trying to sound more confident than I felt.

"Yes," I said softly. "And we will, too."

He frowned, wiped his patch of window clean, and went back to watching the barefoot players disappear into the distance. I noticed his curiosity and his brave attempt to understand this new world. It struck me how strange it must be to arrive somewhere completely unfamiliar and be told, without question, that this is home now.

The van eventually slowed onto a quiet, acacia-lined driveway. As the heavy gates closed behind us, the city's roar was instantly muted. In the Foreign Service, you don't choose your house; it's assigned. I had been given a corner townhouse, beige, glassy, and almost identical to the rest of the compound. But it was clean, secure, and only a seven-minute walk from the USAID office. As the driver opened the door, I realized that while the city outside was a beautiful, tangled web, inside these gates, we had found our landing pad.

I walked into the USAID Mission on my first day dressed for the version of diplomacy I'd seen in movies. I was wearing my best Washington suit, a structured, three-piece affair that screamed "serious professional." Within ten minutes, the Manila heat had turned that suit into a polyester prison. I was drastically overdressed, not just for the tropical climate, but for the reality of my new rank.

I don't know what I expected, perhaps a heavy mahogany desk in a corner office with an oval table for high-level negotiations. Instead, I was led to a small office with a simple computer desk and, interestingly, a love seat on the opposite end.

It was a tiny, intimate space tucked right under a window, a "love nest" with a view of the city that felt far more romantic than my actual job title. Because it had glass walls, there was nowhere to hide my "newbie" status. I was officially a Foreign Service Officer at the starter FS-06 grade.

In the alphabet soup of USAID language, FS-06 is the polite way of saying "Trainee" or "the person who handles the things nobody else wants to touch." I was the lowest-ranking employee on my team, the absolute bottom of a very tall, very intimidating ladder. But as I looked at my small desk and my name on that welcome packet, I didn't care. I was finally on the rungs.

The gravity I had brought with me, that polished, stiff diplomatic tone I'd practiced in D.C., felt suddenly ridiculous. I realized quickly that if I was going to survive the next two years, I had to tone it down. I needed to shed the Washington armor, find a lighter fabric, and join the fun.

As I watched the senior officers walk by with their relaxed confidence and deep portfolios, I realized there were far more levels to this game than I had imagined. I was an FS-06 today, but I wasn't planning on staying one. I was going to climb every inch of this ladder, no matter how many miles or countries they threw at me.

One reason the ladder didn't feel quite so daunting was the man standing at the very top of it. You wouldn't believe who the Ambassador in Manila was: Harry Thomas, Jr. Yes, the same man I had met a few years earlier at a JSI function, the one who had connected me with Alonzo and played a part in opening the doors to USAID in the first place.

I can't describe the surge of joy I felt realizing that at the helm of our diplomatic mission was a man who not only looked like me but had grown up on the very same streets I had. In a world where I was so often "The Other," having an uncle-like figure in the corridors of power made the Philippines feel like the right place at the right time.

I wasn't looking for special treatment; I was still determined to earn my stripes and work my way up. But seeing him there was my daily inspiration. He was the living proof that if it was possible for him, it was possible for me. And it was possible for every other young person from Queens.

I made up my mind right then: I would make the most of this opportunity, no matter how hard it got. I wanted to make sure Ambassador Thomas never regretted opening that door for me. More than that, I wanted to perform so well that the door would stay open for the many others who would come after me.

I often thought about his philosophy on the work we did. He frequently reminded us that "Diplomacy is about people, not just cables." He believed our true strength lay in our diversity and in our ability to connect with the local population on a human level. It was a beautiful, inspiring sentiment.

But being with Ambassador Thomas in the same country also meant I was on high alert. I had to be on my absolute best behavior. I couldn't afford a single slip-up. The last thing I wanted was for someone to walk into his office and say, "You know that girl from Queens you helped out? You won't believe what she just did." Sometimes it felt like I wasn't just working to make a difference or to earn a promotion. I was working to keep the family name clean. I carried that responsibility into every meeting and every field visit.

To this day, I admire Ambassador Thomas's leadership, a leadership that thrived on never leaving anyone behind. He showed me that you could reach the highest corridors of power without losing the "Queens" in your soul. He didn't just hold the door open; he stood there cheering as we walked through. For that, I will forever be grateful.

The embassy in Manila supported a broad, multi-agency mission with hundreds of American staff and thousands of locally employed personnel. On its own, USAID/Philippines managed a wide-ranging portfolio spanning health, governance, the environment, education, and economic growth. One standout initiative launched in 2010 was the "May Plano Ako" national family-planning and behavior-change program. In partnership with the Philippine Department of Health, the HealthPRO project trained hundreds of nurses and thousands of community health workers nationwide in the use of modern contraceptives, helping to frame family planning as a lifestyle choice rather than just a medical service.

Through the Reaching Every Barangay initiative, health teams pushed far beyond clinic walls, traveling into villages spread across dozens of municipalities. In just a few months, thousands of people received preventive care that many had never accessed before. Women began or continued family planning, babies completed their vaccinations, and pregnant mothers finished prenatal visits that could mean the difference between life and loss. But what stayed with me were the moments behind the numbers: a mother hesitating before her first clinic visit, a father listening carefully as he learned how to protect his child's health, a nurse pausing with quiet pride as she recorded another small victory.

Education proved just as powerful as medicine. Mothers gathered in group sessions to talk openly about pregnancy, childbirth, and child health, often replacing fear and rumor with understanding for the first time. Simple, practical materials sparked conversations that rippled through households and communities. Eventually, these approaches were reviewed and endorsed by the Philippine Department of Health, allowing what worked locally to travel nationally and reach families far beyond the places I had visited.

Change was happening inside hospitals, too. New postpartum family planning services and safer childbirth and newborn care practices took root, guided by global standards but shaped by local realities. Behind the scenes, I worked with health leaders to ensure funding actually reached clinics on the ground, helping them stock supplies and keep services running in some of the country's most underserved provinces. Data quietly supported it all, sharpening decisions and revealing where progress was real and where more work was needed. Looking back, I don't remember the spreadsheets as much as the growing confidence of health workers and the relief on parents' faces, signs that health was becoming something people could finally count on.

I quickly learned from our Health Office Director, my new supervisor, Ann, that our office ran programs not only in the Philippines but also across the Pacific. Ann was exceptional, sharp, and compassionate. Under her leadership, I saw what a healthy team truly looked like. I was given responsibility for our HIV portfolio, which felt like starting a whole new chapter, despite the work I had done in the non-profit sector.

Being fully immersed in the health team was a master class in on-the-job learning. Health accounted for the largest share of the Mission portfolio, so every meeting, every project, and every challenge was an opportunity to see development work in motion. Within one year, the Mission expanded from a bilateral to a regional platform, assuming the Pacific Islands program in April 2011. That meant I now had responsibility for an HIV/AIDS project in Papua New Guinea, a country I'd barely known existed, with over 800 indigenous groups and languages and an astonishingly rich culture. I often wondered if I was ready for the challenge of working in two very different countries simultaneously. After all, I was still a newbie.

When most people hear "Papua New Guinea," they aren't thinking about papayas and guinea fowls. I certainly wasn't. I was thinking about the horror stories I'd heard, tribal conflicts, intense violence, and lingering whispers of cannibalism. Honestly? I was terrified.

But the second I stepped onto that first Air Niugini flight, my fear was replaced by a total "mind-blown" moment. I froze in the aisle. The flight attendants had the most perfectly round afros I had ever seen, and their beautiful brown skin glowed flawlessly. Looking at the faces around me, I felt like I had been transported to a village in East Africa that just happened to be in the middle of the Pacific.

How can this place be so far from home, but feel so close? Around these people, I didn't feel like a stranger. I felt like I was among my own.

Landing in Port Moresby, however, was a lesson in diplomatic reality. We didn't actually have a USAID Mission building there; the program was too small. We just had one expat rep and a local assistant tucked into the Embassy. Because there was no desk for me, my "office" was usually a hotel room, and I ventured out only for specific meetings.

The world of Black diplomacy is tiny. As it turned out, the U.S. Ambassador in PNG, Teddy Taylor, was also an African American man and a close friend of Ambassador Thomas. What are the odds? To have these two exemplary leaders at the helm of my first tour, men I could see myself in, was a rare treat. It made the "corridors of power" feel a lot less lonely.

But once I left the capital to monitor our projects, I felt as if I were literally stepping back in time. The countryside was breathtaking, with untouched flora and marine ecosystems that looked as if they belonged in a National Geographic special, but the underdevelopment was staggering.

I'll never forget boarding a domestic flight to Madang. As we stood in line on the tarmac, the airport staff stood at the plane's doorway, casually handing out plastic bags to the passengers, some of whom were boarding completely barefoot.

I nudged my local colleague, the Program Assistant, and whispered, "Wait, why are they giving out trash bags?"

He let out a soft laugh and shook his head. "Look at their feet."

I looked down. An older man just ahead of us, his skin dark and weathered, took his two plastic bags with a nod of thanks. He sat right there on the edge of the stairs, pulled the bags over his feet, which looked as tough and patterned as leather, and began carefully tying the plastic handles around his ankles.

"They are makeshift shoes," my colleague explained softly. "The plane is a 'modern' space, and out of respect for the carpet and the cabin, they cover their feet before they step inside."

I watched the old man stand up, his new "shoes" crinkling against the metal stairs, and step onto the carpeted aisle of the high-tech plane as if it were the most natural thing in the world.

"Only in PNG," my colleague murmured, smiling at my stunned expression.

I realized then that I wasn't just in a different country; I was in a place where the 21st century was still shaking hands with the ancient world. It was a surreal collision of cultures, and it reminded me that if I was going to be successful here, I had to stop looking for things that resembled "home" and start learning the logic of the locals.

That logic applied to the work, too. In Washington, we talked about "strategic interventions," but in the Highlands of PNG, it was about not accidentally starting a riot. We had to be incredibly careful. If we walked into a community and ignored the local leader, or if we appeared to favor one tribe over another with our aid, we weren't just "inefficient"; we were dangerous.

We couldn't just show up with a clipboard and a "DC-approved" solution. I had to listen first. If the community didn't feel empowered to find its own path to stability, then all the funding in the world wouldn't matter. It was a delicate dance of trying to support people without stepping on the very traditions that held them together.

Some of my work in the Philippines took me far beyond Manila, making it feel like it was a whole other country sometimes, too. The first time I was told I would be traveling to Mindanao in the south, I recall sitting through a security briefing with the Embassy's Regional Affairs Officer, trying to appear composed as they outlined the risks.

Mindanao has always been the Philippines's rebellious southern frontier: a single island wearing two faces. I saw emerald ridges plunging toward beaches so white they were blinding, and clouds braiding above volcanoes while hornbills flared across the canopy. In the valley towns below, I knew a church bell was likely swinging just one beat behind the call to prayer blaring from a minaret's loudspeaker.

Yet, as I quickly learned, beauty here carries counterbalance.

Since the seventies, those same forests have hidden rebel camps, those same coastlines have smuggled arms, and those same crossroads have hosted checkpoints where soldiers scan faces for yesterday's wanted poster. The island's loveliness is never separate from its ledger of grievances; paradise here keeps a running tally of disappearances.

"Mindanao isn't like Manila," the Regional Security Officer said, his voice flat as he tapped a finger on a map of the southern Philippines. "We call these 'non-permissive environments.' And by that I mean there's active fighting on the ground."

I sat there in the briefing room, trying to look like a composed Foreign Service Officer while my stomach did somersaults. Up until that point, my biggest concern was the humidity ruining my suit. Now, I was told that "safe" was officially negotiable.

"You'll be in a military aircraft," he continued, glancing at me to see if I was tracking. "Armored vehicles only. And you don't move an inch without a shadow. Not even to cross a courtyard to get a bottle of water. Understood?"

"Understood," I said, my voice steadier than I felt.

The first time I strapped into a heavy bulletproof vest and pulled on a helmet, I felt like I was playing a character in a movie. I'd never worked this closely with the military before, and watching their precision was an education. Every step was a calculation; every route was checked and triple-checked.

"Stay close, Ma'am," one of the guys whispered as we moved toward an armored SUV. "We've got eyes on everything."

Was I scared? Absolutely. But as we rattled over the broken roads toward a small rural health clinic, the adrenaline gave way to the beat of the mission.

When the heavy doors of the vehicle finally opened, the "chaos" of the security warnings disappeared. I stepped into a modest clinic where the air was still and smelled of antiseptic. Inside, I didn't see insurgents or "threats"; I saw nurses and doctors.

They looked just like medical staff anywhere else in the world, battling the same old enemies: limited resources, a line of patients out the door, and a budget that never quite stretched far enough. But they beamed with pride and determination to serve their community the best way they could.

In that quiet clinic, the armor suddenly felt too heavy. The real battles weren't out in the jungle. They were right here, in the daily, stubborn fight to keep people healthy. And I was honored to be part of it.

When I first arrived in Manila, I didn't fully comprehend that I was stepping into one of the busiest posts in the world, where every single US federal agency was represented.

One of those agencies was my beloved Peace Corps. As a former volunteer, working in a country with an active program was a dream come true. The bonus? The Peace Corps Country Director was also Haitian-American. In the small world of Black diplomacy, it was another remarkable coincidence. We quickly grew close, and outside the office, our families blended socially as if we'd known each other back in New York. I helped negotiate an interagency agreement to support their HIV/AIDS work, and watching Peace Corps volunteers like Phil and Alex present their projects reminded me that even the smallest interventions can ripple out across an entire province.

While the field was about healing communities, the Manila office became an unexpected place for a different kind of healing. My tiny "love nest" office had a small seat under the window that, without my intending it, became like a therapist's couch. Colleagues would drop by, close the door, and talk. I'd listen as they decompressed about work or life, and soon the office joke was that I had a side gig as a counselor. My personality tests always said I should be a social worker or a teacher; it turns out I found a way to do both without ever changing my job title.

But if my office were the therapy room, the conference room was the soul of the Mission. Filipinos don't just work; they perform. Every birthday or promotion was a Broadway-level production, complete with karaoke and dance skits. There was a genuine warmth there, and a sense of family that made the demanding red-alert taskers from Washington feel manageable.

The most sacred rule of all? Lunch. At twelve-thirty sharp, the work stopped.

I'd be buried in procurement checklists when a head would pop into my office: "Food, Ma'am."

That was the command to drop everything. We'd migrate to the conference room, pushing aside project folders to make way for foil pans of *pancit*, leaking bags of adobo, and steaming rice. If you showed up empty-handed, a plate would magically appear for you. Those thirty minutes felt like a weekend. It was a beautiful, human rhythm, until the ground itself decided to join the conversation.

I remember my first earthquake vividly. We were mid-lunch when the room began to sway. My chest tightened; I couldn't tell if it was the building or my heart shaking.

I looked around, waiting for the screaming to start, but nobody moved. My colleagues just set their utensils down and watched their plates shift a few inches to the left.

"What's happening?" I managed to choke out, halfway to diving under the heavy mahogany table.

Without looking up from her rice, Marichi, the matriarch and longest serving member of the team, said, "Don't worry, it's just an earthquake." Then she went right back to her lunch.

Just like that, it was over. I sat there, stunned, while they continued their conversation as if nothing had happened. For them, it wasn't a disaster; it was just Tuesday.

Back at the townhouse, my mother worked her quiet magic. She reestablished her small empire faster than I could unpack; curtains were hung, and pans were aligned within a week. Anthony, at seven, was taking it all in with wide-eyed wonder, though his adjustment was a bit of a slow burn. The Manila traffic was unforgiving, and his commute to the international school took nearly an hour each way. "He just sleeps on the bus, Ma'am," the matron would assure me. "No worries."

Between embassy functions and family-friendly gatherings at Ambassador Thomas's residence, our social calendar was full. We found a spiritual home at *Santuario de San Antonio*, where Anthony took his First Holy Communion. But even in paradise, some new family challenges emerged.

Midway through that first year, Anthony's teacher called a meeting. "He's a joy to have in class," she said gently, "but he struggles to stay on task."

I wasn't entirely surprised, given his speech delays back in the U.S., but it still felt like a punch to the gut. During our next trip home, we got the diagnosis: ADHD, the inattentive type. Suddenly, the "dreamy" kid who slept on the bus made sense. We hired a local tutor named Thomas back in Manila, a man with the patience of a saint, who helped Anthony find the tools to navigate his own mind.

But while the classroom was a struggle, the basketball court was his kingdom.

Anthony had loved the game since Maryland, and soon I found myself with a brand-new identity: Basketball Mom. I was in the rotation for snacks, team fundraisers, and carpools. The court became our sanctuary, a place where the "Foreign Service" labels fell away.

Even my mother found peace there. She'd sit on the sidelines, smiling as the boys darted up and down the court. Watching Anthony play, I realized that adapting to a new culture wasn't just about surviving earthquakes; it was about growing in the unexpected gaps between work and home.

What really made settling into Manila brilliant was the visit from my sister Nancy and my cousin Stephanie. I still remember when we all decided to head to the beach. We did it the local way by piling into two motorized trikes, or tuk tuks as they are commonly called. Now, I am not the most adventurous person, and these things were basically tiny three-wheeled tricycle taxis. They felt so light that I was convinced a stiff breeze could toss us right over. Our driver wove through the thick traffic like a pro, darting into gaps that looked barely wide enough for a bicycle and leaning into every turn while we gripped the sides for dear life. Against all odds, we made it to the famed Boracay beach in one piece.

The beach was a stretch of blinding white sand that seemed to glow against the turquoise water. Nancy, Stephanie, and I stood there together looking out at a horizon so clear it felt like you could see the edge of the world. Nearby, my mother sat under the shade of a palm tree watching over Anthony. He was completely lost in his own world, digging into the sand. Local kids ran by and stopped to watch him with wide eyes and bright smiles, but Anthony didn't mind. He just kept playing and fitting in perfectly.

We spent the afternoon sipping on cold Buko juice straight out of the coconuts, eating the most divine mangoes and exotic fresh fruits, and laughing as the sun dipped lower. Seeing us all there, New York girls and a young boy in the middle of a Philippine island, grounded me. It was those raw and unscripted moments that made me realize I wasn't just working in the Philippines. I was actually living there. It made me love the place even more.

But everything wasn't perfect. Is anything in life?

Being a Black family in Manila meant we were often the subject of intense curiosity. I remember a trip to the massive Mall of Asia that turned sour in a heartbeat. I was standing in line to pay for my items, and Anthony was sitting nearby on the edge of a display table.

Out of the corner of my eye, I saw a saleslady approaching him. I didn't think much of it at first; people were generally friendly. But then she reached out. She started touching his head, feeling his hair as if he were an exhibit in a petting zoo. I didn't hesitate. I moved swiftly, pulling Anthony away and looking her dead in the eye.

"Don't you ever touch my child again," I told her, my voice sharp enough to cut.

Anthony looked confused, the lady scurried away in a panic, and I was absolutely livid. I paid for my items with shaking hands and got us home as fast as I could. I don't know what her intentions were, curiosity, fascination, whatever, but I knew one thing for sure: my child wasn't going to be treated like an attraction. Not on my watch.

But for every person who reached out to touch Anthony's hair, there was another who reached out to offer a hand in friendship. I realized that if I spent all my time being a shield, I'd never have my hands free to actually embrace the life we were building.

So, I leaned back into the warmth I had come to love.

I also found a world outside the Embassy gates. I made friends with people like Desta, a beautiful Eritrean singer I'd met through the local live music scene. Through friendships like that and our family vacations to places like Cebu, Boracay, and Palawan, I saw the country's landscapes at their absolute best.

When the reassignment notice arrived from Washington, I wasn't prepared. *Had two years really gone by already?* We were starting to fall in love with mango desserts. I was mastering enough Tagalog phrases to truly impress my counterparts. It was all happening too fast. I sat in my office, gazing at the small love seat where so many colleagues had shared their stories, and I thought, *Not yet.* Manila had become home. The people had become family. Even the heat, once so unbearable, had started to feel like comfort.

I realized then that the most critical turns in life aren't always the ones we choose. South Africa hadn't been my first choice for the Peace Corps, yet it became a defining chapter of my life. The Philippines wasn't on my wish list either, but I had ended up exactly where I needed to be, serving under a mentor who had set my whole career in motion.

Maybe that's the real lesson of the Foreign Service: you don't always choose the path, but if you're open to it, the unplanned route leads you exactly where you're supposed to be.

Papua New Guinea site visit and focus group discussion.

Taking a military helicopter ride with my colleagues Dion and Lee for a site visit in Jolo.

Chapter Ten

WHERE THE OCEAN MET MY RHYTHM

If the ocean and the savanna ever had a child," my coworker Judy from the Manila office had joked before I left, "they'd name her Tanzania."

Looking out the airplane window, I realized that even that was an understatement. Mount Kilimanjaro filled the frame, a massive crater rising straight through the clouds, snow-capped and gleaming against the blue.

I leaned aside so Mom and Anthony could catch glimpses out the window. The mountain caught the light and glimmered like a shining star. It felt more like a spiritual homecoming than an arrival. Then the cabin door opened, and the heat rushed in before we could even step outside.

Inside Julius Nyerere International Airport, the reality was different from what I'd imagined. Despite being in the heart of East Africa, I stepped into a terminal packed with tourists carrying hiking backpacks and missionary workers in cargo pants and Birkenstock sandals. I paused, struck by how few faces looked like mine. Fair-haired adults in multi-pocketed safari vests moved through the space with extreme confidence. I'd crossed an ocean looking for mirrored images, only to find the familiar outlines of the West dominating the room.

We proceeded to the Immigration section and entered the expedited lane reserved for diplomats and UN officials. Standing there with our American passports and Western suitcases, even the airport staff's stares seemed to ask a silent question: *Are you really supposed to be in that VIP line, or are you lost?* I picked my head up and kept it moving because this wasn't the first time my belonging would be questioned.

"Karibuni sana, Dada. Welcome home." I was relieved to hear the embassy driver's voice as we reached the other side of the queue.

He grabbed our bags, and we followed him out of the air-conditioned terminal and into the thick, humid embrace of Dar es Salaam's heat. The airport was neat and orderly, with parking lots laid out with modern precision that rivaled any international hub. We settled into the car, closing the doors against the humid air, and merged onto the main road.

Wide, smoothly paved roads extended ahead, flanked by towering billboards that dominated the horizon. Neatly trimmed shrubs lined the sides, while clusters of palm trees in the center swayed gently in the breeze. It gave the impression of a city swiftly advancing into the future.

Then the polished version gave out.

As we headed toward the heart of the city, the wide lanes gently narrowed, and we hit the city's true pulse. Traffic slowed to a crawl. The lush greenery gave way to the industrial hum of factories. The manicured bushes vanished, replaced by endless rows of tented structures stretching for miles. They reminded me of the spaza shops in South Africa, though these were crafted from rough canvas and adorned with bright umbrellas. It was a bustling marketplace, alive with energy and excitement.

Stuck in that traffic, my world narrowed to a small stall on the roadside. A young woman, barely an adult, hunched over a steaming pot with a baby tied securely to her back in a colorful wrap. Beside her, a young girl worked with focused, rapid movements. She looked about nine years old, the same age as Anthony.

I looked at the girl, then at Anthony, sitting comfortably in the air-conditioned backseat, his fingers tracing the leather of his basketball. He worried about nothing more than the scuff on his sneakers.

Through the tinted glass, I watched her. I realized she was the very person I was here to fight for. To the office, she was the 'Strategic Information' I had to manage, but to me, she was the entire reason I had come to Tanzania. She was the youth bulge that demographers warn about, the inequality, the maternal health statistic, all in one small, determined frame.

I leaned closer to the glass and whispered, "I'm here for you."

By the time we reached our new house, I could still see the girl's face. The next morning, as I walked into the USAID mission for orientation, I wasn't just looking at a new office. I was looking for a way to reach her.

Tanzania was a country of breathtaking beauty with some striking contradictions. On one hand, it was a world-class tourist destination for very good reasons. In the north, Arusha and Moshi sit beneath the watchful grace of Mount Meru and Kilimanjaro, where mornings are cool and green, scented with coffee and rain, and the air feels full of possibility. Westward, Mwanza, also known as Rock City, rises along the shores of Lake Victoria, its giant boulders stacked like ancient sculptures, fishermen moving quietly through pink dawns as the lake breathes and shimmers. Down south, the Southern Highlands of Mbeya and Iringa roll out in deep greens and misty blues across expansive tea fields, red earth, crisp air, and a stillness that settles into your bones and slows your spirit. And then there is the coast, Pemba and Kilwa, warm and salt-kissed, where the Indian Ocean glows turquoise, palm trees sway lazily, and history lingers in coral stone and sea breezes.

On the other hand, it faced significant inequality. Half the population lived on less than a dollar a day. Thirty dollars a month, meant to cover food, rent, transport, and school fees, was an entire family's lifeline. Back home, that amount barely paid for a casual lunch for two.

The "youth bulge" was not just a term from a textbook. When more than 44 percent of the population is under fifteen, you see it everywhere. For most families, the choice was not about which school to attend. Instead, they worried if they could even afford a uniform or a single notebook. As a result, nearly half of those children struggled to read a basic sentence. These were not just statistics. They were the nation's future.

Inequality fell hardest on women, girls, and marginalized groups like the LGBTQ+ population. For many women, childbirth remained the greatest risk they would ever face. A lack of transportation and outdated gender roles only made this danger worse. The struggle for contraception was equally staggering. One in four married women who wanted to avoid pregnancy simply could not get it.

When I joined the health team, I took on a new role leading the formation of our Strategic Information (SI) team. We managed the data for all our health programs. With forty-two colleagues, we focused on building relationships with key stakeholders and targeting root causes. Like the Philippines, our programs covered HIV, family planning, and maternal and child health. However, we also tackled malaria. I admit I was not an expert, as I had not worked directly in SI before.

On my first day, a wave of self-doubt hit me. I wondered how I could lead a team focused on a technical workstream that felt so unfamiliar. However, our Office Director saw my management skills as the missing piece needed to build the team from the ground up. I jumped in. I originally hoped to join the HIV prevention team because it was my passion, dating back to my time in the Peace Corps. Still, I was determined to make the most of this new challenge. I worked with two incredible Tanzanian colleagues and connected with brilliant minds at the National Bureau of Statistics. Those relationships changed everything for me. They deepened my understanding of data and gave me a genuine appreciation for how it drives impact.

About a year later, I became the Lead for the HIV Prevention team and supervised a staff of five. That is when I began working on Gender-Based Violence (GBV), a major issue in Tanzania. Eventually, I was named the Gender-Based Violence Initiative Coordinator for the PEPFAR interagency team. I was no longer that wide-eyed trainee or the newcomer trying to find her footing. I was leading teams and sitting at tables with the CDC, the Department of Defense, and the State Department. I felt like I finally had the reins.

But just as I stepped into this leadership role, the political climate turned volatile. The U.S. Government's relationship with Tanzania fundamentally changed after their 2015 presidential election. The new Tanzanian administration moved toward authoritarian policies almost overnight. The atmosphere became heavy and unpredictable. Suddenly, our work was not just about health; it was about navigating a minefield.

The government began raiding our partners' offices and accusing them of promoting homosexuality. They even restricted travel for officials, which made our daily collaboration feel like pulling teeth. I realized then that the support we brought to these communities would never be smooth sailing. It was a brutal lesson in how quickly politics can disrupt and dismantle progress.

The persecution escalated in ways that defied all public health logic. The government started confiscating condoms and lubricants, which are fundamental and critical tools for HIV prevention. They forcibly shut down drop-in centers. Those centers were the only safe spaces where LGBTQ+ individuals could get care without being targeted.

It became personal very quickly. I started hearing stories about friends I had met through my outreach work. These were good people, dedicated people, and now they were in hiding or fleeing the country to save their lives. The fear was constant, and it kept pulling my mind back to our colleague, Xulhaz Mannan.

Xulhaz was a tireless advocate for minority rights in Bangladesh and a beloved member of our USAID family. Only a year earlier, attackers had entered his home and murdered him for defending the rights of minorities. His death stayed with me like a shadow because it exposed a terrifying truth: the work we were doing wasn't just fighting a virus; it was fighting a deep-rooted, global belief system that viewed certain lives as disposable.

Outside the political arena, we dealt with a range of deep-rooted issues. One of my greatest passions was empowering young girls. Tanzania, like many other countries, struggled with the culture of child marriage. We were constantly walking a tightrope. On one hand, we had to respect thousand-year-old cultural practices.

On the other hand, we had a responsibility to protect the rights of girls and women. It was a delicate, often exhausting balance. We had to find ways to move forward without tearing the social fabric apart.

The most challenging aspect was female genital mutilation (FGM), a gender-based violence issue closely linked to child marriages. It wasn't just a tradition; It came down to family honor and financial survival. For these households, a daughter's "purity" determined her worth and their future.

A colleague from the Ministry of Health once showed me a map marked with red districts where "FGM season" began with the new moon. She told me how grandmothers would pay the cutters in chickens. She told me about girls who resisted, only to have their own aunts drag them away. These aunts had survived the same mutilation decades before and now enforced it as a non-negotiable rite of passage.

These weren't just traditions; they were survival strategies and deep-seated secrets. Other stories were quieter but just as devastating.

I'll never forget a young girl in a classroom, while we were on a site visit, who once courageously shared with a group of us, "Please don't tell my mother, but my cousin forces himself on me." It was heartbreaking to see the terror in her eyes. It reminded me that for every public ritual, there were a thousand private violences.

Our biggest discussion always came back to the same point: how do we change a belief system that takes control of a woman's body before she can even claim it for herself?

One thing was clear: to move this community forward, we had to prioritize education, especially for girls. Of course, we had initiatives for men and boys, too, but the barriers for girls were unique and deeply entrenched.

Educating a girl child was not a simple "get the girls to school" problem; it was an economic and cultural puzzle. For most families, a daughter was a source of income. Marrying her off brought in cash or livestock, which provided a lifeline for a struggling business or a hungry household.

Our first solution, built on direct community input, addressed those economic roots. In rural areas, child marriage was often a survival strategy, one less mouth to feed. To counter this, we started offering livestock and cash transfers to families who kept their daughters in school. We had to prove that a girl's education was worth more to the family's long-term survival than an early marriage bed would be in the short term.

Second, we reached out to the men. We knew we could not move the needle by talking only to women. We recruited men to be "champions", male peer educators who challenged the very norms they had been raised to protect. It was a massive mind-shift. When fathers and brothers began to value the dignity of their daughters and sisters, the entire dynamic changed. We also enlisted community and religious leaders, hoping they could lend their influential voices to the cause.

We even worked with elders to create new rites of passage. These new ceremonies honored their heritage and marked the transition to adulthood without the use of a blade. We were not fighting their culture. Instead, we were giving them a choice and a way to protect their children without losing their identity.

I also dove into the "Let Girls Learn" initiative. In Tanzania, only 24 percent of adolescent girls were in school. That was a crisis we simply could not ignore. I joined the design team to lead a massive gender assessment with the host government, local counterparts, and U.S. government colleagues. We used an "innovative co-creation" approach. That is a fancy way of saying we actually sat everyone down in the same room, from the Washington staff and the local embassy to our international and local partners. We built the program together from the ground up. Eventually, we launched a six-million-dollar project designed to break down the barriers keeping those girls out of the classroom.

Around that same time, I took the lead on the Young African Leaders Initiative, or YALI. I worked directly with YALI alums and used their technical expertise to pivot our programs. We stopped just "planning for" youth and started "planning with" them. At USAID, we created an Advisory Council for the first time, and I ensured YALI alumni like Geline, a brilliant legal expert, joined. It was a massive effort that required me to engage with senior government officials and civil society leaders.

After years of pushing for evidence-informed advocacy with Washington, we finally launched the PEPFAR DREAMS initiative. The name alone stood for everything these girls deserved: Determined, Resilient, Empowered, AIDS-Free, Mentored, and Safe.

For the first time, we stopped trying to squeeze these girls into our policy boxes. Instead, we started meeting them where they actually stood. We realized that a girl does not stay HIV-free just because a nurse tells her to be careful. She stays safe when she has a reason to hope, the resources to survive, and the power to protect her own dreams.

It was a massive, multi-layered effort. If a girl was at risk, we didn't just give her a brochure. We provided a peer mentor who looked like her. We gave her a safe space to talk about her body. We helped her family secure small-business grants so they wouldn't feel pressured to marry her off for a dowry. We even partnered with heavyweights like Nike and the Gates Foundation to bring private-sector innovations, bringing in resources that made the program feel and look aspirational rather than strictly clinical.

I remember walking into one of our community safe spaces and seeing a circle of teenage girls, the same age as the one who had whispered to me in the classroom. But here, the energy was different. They weren't whispering; they were debating, planning, and laughing. They were becoming the authors of their own stories.

The real turning point, though, appeared in the data. Within just one year, we saw new HIV infections among adolescent girls drop by eighteen percent. After so many long months of fighting the tide, I finally felt a wave of hope.

I looked at those spreadsheets and didn't just see percentages; I saw the face of the young girl I had seen from the car window on my first day in Dar es Salaam. For once, the numbers had the same eyes as the girls I saw in the streets. Those faces were no longer just "Strategic Information" we had to manage or statistics to track. They were looking toward a future they finally owned.

While we fought these heavy battles, other workstreams provided much-needed levity. We promoted the country's most popular condom brand, Dume, through a social marketing project. We hosted activation events in non-traditional venues, including sports events and music festivals. We even created *Siri ya Mtungi* (Secrets of the Pot), which became the country's most popular television drama series. It raised awareness about family planning and HIV prevention through storytelling.

We collaborated with Swahiliwood filmmakers to produce health education films, which culminated in a full red-carpet event where I got to pretend to be a star with work friends like Flo and Alicia, two firebrands who brought a lot of energy in and out of the office. It was a reminder that health work can be vibrant and celebratory, too.

One of my proudest moments involved working with Dr. Grace Mallya, the gender focal person at the Ministry of Health. She was a true champion, but government restrictions made it almost impossible for her to travel. I didn't want the world to hear about Tanzania from a report; I wanted them to hear it from her. Through some persistent advocacy, we finally cleared the way for her to speak at a global conference in Washington, D.C. She was the only government voice there. Seeing her share the local realities of our work on a global stage proved that local voices, with the lived experiences, are the most powerful tools we have.

With all of that, the work on gender-based violence remained the hardest. Near the end of my time in Tanzania, I was proud of what we achieved. We expanded our services, secured more funding, and helped establish one-stop centers at police stations for survivors in major cities nationwide.

The ironic thing about gender-based violence and discrimination is that it is a plague we have to keep fighting on every level. In Tanzania, it wore an ugly, obvious face. But as I continued my work, I realized that the same violence permeates every facet of society, even in the developed world. It just hides better there.

At the office, more specifically when interacting with other officers at the Embassy, I began encountering a different kind of resistance and intolerance than I had experienced in the Philippines. Diplomatic postings often pose an unspoken challenge to inclusion for people of color. You often find yourself in places where you don't quite fit in, or where you're the only face that looks like yours. In these high-level circles, discrimination is often subtly masked by professional protocols. Professional isolation grows from a subtle discomfort around you, you feel the temperature shift when you speak, you notice how support thins and scrutiny sharpens. You might face a lack of support or even outright resistance to your presence and your ascent.

I never confused those moments with the gender-based violence our clients endured. Their suffering was immediate, physical, and devastating in ways I would never claim as my own. But I began to understand that the forces at work were related. The dismissal of women of color in a boardroom and the abuse of women in a rural village grow from the same belief system. One operates in whispers, the other in blows, but both rest on the idea that certain women can be diminished, ignored, or controlled. Naming that connection did not lessen the gravity of their pain; it clarified why the work mattered so deeply to me.

That is why it is such a blessing when another woman stands up for you. To arrive in a place like that and find a senior leader who not only looks like you but also has your back is rare. It is a gift.

I found that bonus in our Mission Director. She was sharp, confident, and always supportive. She had decades of experience and a real talent for identifying people's strengths. I remember a moment before an important briefing when I was feeling nervous. She walked over to me, calm and steady.

"You have got this," she said. "Just focus on the key points. Remember, nobody knows this data better than you."

Her confidence rubbed off on me. I went in and presented well because she reminded me of my own expertise. She championed women's empowerment and ensured we had the opportunity to lead. I know I would not have earned my first real promotion without her mentorship.

Looking back, those years in Tanzania felt like being thrown into the deep end of international development. I saw firsthand the heavy weight these communities carry every day. My work took me into the heart of the most difficult human struggles.

Yet through it all, dedicated teams and local communities stood with us, giving their all to the mission every single day. They refused to let the hostility or their disadvantages stop them from saving lives. I had seen the agility of the human spirit before, back in South Africa. In Tanzania, I saw it once again. I witnessed the resistance and the sheer will it takes to keep standing when things turn south.

Without even noticing, I was also learning how to keep standing. I was learning what it takes to remain upright even when your own bones start to fail you. Their resilience was infectious. Amid those challenges, I realized I was growing in ways I never expected. I was no longer just watching from the sidelines. I was mastering the data, leading the teams, and finding my voice in the work I loved most. I was becoming the leader I once only dreamed of being.

Being interviewed on the Swahiliwood red carpet to showcase our health education films

Chapter Eleven

WHAT I COULDN'T HOLD ON TO

When I moved to Dar es Salaam, life felt both expansive and grounding. I stepped into a new leadership role at USAID and began the adventure of raising my son in a country that vibrated with energy. Living on the Swahili coast meant opening myself to a life that felt familiar and brand new, all at once. The pace of the city seemed to whisper, "Relax. You're home now."

And relax, I did. I traded my fast-paced Western expectations for a "*pole pole*" state of mind. We spent our weekends letting the Indian Ocean wash away the stress of the work week. I remember the smell of mishkaki beef grilling on street corners and the way the call to prayer drifted over the city, blending with the rhythm of Bongo Flava music. Even though I served as an American diplomat, I didn't feel like a visitor. I felt like I had finally reclaimed a piece of myself that I didn't even know was missing.

Anthony was thriving, too. Moving to a new country is hard on a kid, but before long, he was starting basketball games at my friend Cray's training camp, trying out Swahili words, and collecting friends like baseball cards. Hailing from Cote d'Ivoire, Cray is married to my friend Jackie who also was a Peace Corps Volunteer in South Africa, a few years after me, and also used to work at Africare, a few years after me. Watching Anthony navigate this world with the same ease he had back home made me realize that "home" isn't a coordinate on a map. It's a feeling of belonging. For the first time in a long time, my soul felt completely at rest.

It was lovely to host Nancy and Stephanie once again, this time in Tanzania. I love how they became a traveling duo. Even though I told them I was happy, I think they needed to see it with their own eyes to really believe I was fine. Having them there, seeing my new life and how much we had settled in, felt like a final stamp of approval. Their visit was a beautiful reminder that no matter how far I travel, my core family will always find a way to reach me.

My mother, as usual, anchored us. There was always a warm breakfast in the morning and something hot in the oven in the evening. Coming home to her cooking was a blessing I looked forward to every day. It turns out I wasn't the only one. Anyone who came even a mile close to our home became a regular; my mom's cooking had that kind of pull. She had a way she cooked chicken in a tomato baste that made it fall off the bones every single time and made it finger-licking good. Then there was Anthony's favorite, eggplant *legume* with rice.

We hosted dinners that stretched late into the night, where the conversation flowed easily. Before long, I started building and expanding my Dar community. In the beginning, Debra and Latrice at the Embassy were my constants. They worked for the U.S. Embassy in a different building, but we hung out together so much you would have thought we shared an office. Someone started calling us the Three Musketeers, and it fit perfectly. We were inseparable. We moved beyond being colleagues and became a chosen family.

We became regulars at so many spots that the owners welcomed us like family. Soon, every joint we frequented knew us by name. They would instinctively reserve a table for us even if we didn't call. They guided us to the same corner table with its little "reserved" sign and let the night take over. Sometimes we danced until our feet hurt. Every few songs, someone would raise a glass and shout, "To surviving another week!" It was a toast that always felt like a victory. Other times we'd get the best massages and mani/pedis from Christina's Zen Spa to melt the stress away.

The Masaki neighborhood in Dar es Salaam has this strip of outdoor bars and restaurants right next to the beach. You have the streets and the city behind you, and the ocean right in front of you. It felt like walking into a portal. Triniti was one of our favorite spots, half indoors, half open to the stars. On nights with a live band or a DJ, you could hear the music, the laughter, and your own pulse all at once.

Another blessing in Dar is the large expat community. Around that time, I was meeting people and making connections everywhere. I never said "no" to a new introduction. I was truly excited about and open to all possibilities. I helped establish one of the first organized Black diaspora groups in Dar, along with friends like Gaidi, Anike, and Ranahnah, who were also working in Tanzania at the time. The group united African Americans, Afro-Caribbeans, and Africans from across the continent. We gathered for potlucks, game nights, and deep conversations about identity, belonging, and what it means to feel at home far from where you were born.

Through that group, I met legends. I met Mama C and Baba Pete, old-school civil rights warriors and Black Panthers now living quietly and building community in Arusha. I met David Robinson, son of the baseball star Jackie Robinson, who owns coffee farms in Mbeya. Somewhere along the way, as I kept meeting more and more people, my friend Jean, also from Queens, jokingly started calling me the "Mayor" of Dar es Salaam, and it stuck.

I'll never forget the days I met Joe and Shamsa. To be more specific, Joe is Joe *Legendary* from Moshi. He was already called that in his early twenties, and for good reason. As a national radio personality, his voice and presence could command a room before he even said a word. And then there was Shamsa, a soft-spoken powerhouse who worked at the embassy. Her poems could hush a crowd, and her discipline kept our dreams from crumbling under the weight of disorganization.

I didn't know it then, but those two plus Gaidi were the team that would eventually help me build a community legacy from the ground up.

They quickly became like the younger siblings I never had. We had a lot of fun together, but more importantly, we took care of each other.

One Thanksgiving, we hosted a cultural exchange dinner with friends from near and far, where everyone cooked dishes from their home countries. It quickly turned into a spice contest nobody wanted to lose. Beza would bring the best Ethiopian *tibs* and Supa would bring his popular Tanzanian *mbuzi*. Times like that felt like magic. They taught me, most simply, that home is the people you laugh with, not a place on a map. I still carry that with me.

For one of my birthdays, our whole motley crew, including Neil, a finance guru, and Mejah, an old school graffiti legend, stayed out until the sky began to lighten. We drove to Coco Beach, half-delirious, watching the black sky turn purple, then pink. Joe and I flopped onto the sand and waited for the sun. Gaidi started doing push-ups.

"This is stupid," I said. "I should be in bed."

Joe shrugged. "Then you'd miss this."

He was right. It was the best sunrise I ever witnessed.

But as much as I loved the energy of the city at dawn, there was only one place I couldn't get enough of. Have you ever felt so connected to a place that you swore you'd settle there? For me, that place was Zanzibar.

The beach in Nungwi swept me off my feet. The powdery sand felt like sifted sugar under my toes, stretching toward waters so clear they hardly seemed real. Most days, the ocean shifted through shades of pale aqua and deep turquoise, like watching a painter blend colors in slow motion. I would float on the surface for what felt like forever, letting the sea's calm soothe something deep within me.

Then there was Stone Town, with its history and heartbeat. Every meal tasted like a love letter: pilau, chapati, and samaki infused with spices grown in the island's own soil.

Wandering the narrow cobblestone streets felt like stepping into a storybook written in carved wooden doors and weathered stone arches. I'd slip my hand into that of a local henna artist, watching swirling patterns emerge on my skin that connected me to the island's creative pulse. I told everyone I would retire there someday. It became a running joke. Whenever the pressure of the mission felt like too much, I'd say to myself, "Just a few more weeks until I can be barefoot in Nungwi."

As beautiful as the turquoise waters of Zanzibar are, they take on a different glow when you have the right person by your side. I had my friends and family, but I found myself longing for a partner to share quiet moments with. When I finally found that person, Zanzibar was the only place that felt grand enough to hold what we were building.

Now, I know what you are thinking: *Wait, here comes another misfit.*

Believe me, he was far from a misfit. Walking the narrow streets of Stone Town with him felt like we were the only two people in the storybook. We'd kick off our shoes and walk barefoot, side by side, feeling the cool, ancient stone beneath our feet and the salt air on our skin. We watched the sunset from the beach in Nungwi, our shadows stretching long over the sand, and for the first time, I wasn't just dreaming of retirement. I was living a life that felt completely whole.

But before we were walking the beaches of Zanzibar, we were just two people navigating the humidity and chaos of daily life in Dar.

You see, when I fall for someone, I typically go all in. I'm not a casual dating person. I was about a decade past my divorce, running the usual mom relay: school drop-off, practice, work, repeat. Then

151

one afternoon, I looked up from the bleachers and saw one of Anthony's sports coaches smiling at the kids. Everything slowed down for a second. I checked quickly and there was no wedding band. He was strikingly handsome, with light brown skin, dark hair, and a fit, athletic build. He had a bit of "Mr. Cool" about him, without arrogance.

At first, we just exchanged polite hellos. Before we knew it, we were dating. My mother, who side-eyes every man within a mile of me, liked him right away. He teased her softly, fixed her chair, and made a big fuss about her cooking. She relaxed, which was a first. Anthony didn't even blink. Coach was already the guy who passed him the ball and told him to stop traveling. Seeing him on our couch felt normal. Anthony would just say, "Hey, Coach," and keep doing his homework.

Somehow, without planning it, he became part of our daily life. We started taking trips together: Seychelles, Dubai, and, of course, Zanzibar. Our trip to the private island of Fanjove was one of our best. It felt like we were totally in sync. I booked the flights and hotels just like I always do. His coaching salary was more about passion than money, so I covered the big stuff and didn't complain. He picked up dinners when he could and brought groceries. It felt fair enough.

Then came that one New Year's in Zanzibar.

Zanzibar is my reset button. On paper, this trip should have been magic: sunsets, music, and champagne at midnight. It wasn't. He was there with me, but his phone got more of his attention than I did. New Year's Eve, sitting across from the man I love, I watched him grin at a screen. It made me wonder who he was really showing up for.

I finally spoke up. We argued, and the weekend turned awkward.

We had tickets to see a singer I knew from back home, and even she leaned over in the van ride afterward to whisper, "You two okay?"

I laughed it off, but inside, I was furious. I had paid for

practically every part of this weekend so we could be together, and he couldn't put his phone down. Why did he even agree to it? Looking back, there were flags, but I chose to keep giving my all.

The real wake-up call came from another young man who often hung around Anthony's games. He had been circling me for months, and I finally mentioned that I was dating Coach to shut him down.

He gave me a slow smile, like I'd told a joke. "Oh. You're with him."

"Yes. And it's serious, so I don't want any problems. Okay?"

"You know," he said, "there are some things you might not know about your guy. Ask him if he has kids."

My stomach tightened. There's no way, I thought. A few days later, at his place, the words finally came out. I couldn't hold it in anymore.

"Hey. Crazy question. Do you have any kids?"

"What?" He paused. "Who told you that?"

"That doesn't matter. Well, do you?"

He looked at me for a long second, the "Mr. Cool" mask finally slipping. "Yes," he said softly. "Now I do. I have a daughter on the way."

On the way. The words hit me like a physical blow. In my mind, I should have been doing the math. I should have been counting back the months, asking for dates, and demanding a timeline.

But I didn't ask how many months. I didn't do the math. I didn't want to.

I was so "all in" that I chose to protect the dream instead of the truth. He claimed his ex got pregnant before we ever met, and he didn't want to "chase me away" by telling me.

I decided to keep going, accepting his version because "life happens." I convinced myself that even if my romantic foundation was shaky, my house was still solid. I still had my community, my work, and most importantly, my mother. I figured my family would fill the gaps that he couldn't.

But while I was busy trying to find my rhythm in the city, a shift was happening at home that I didn't see coming.

I started to notice a few glitches in my mom's behavior. Sometimes she would forget what I had just told her or completely forget where she left her keys. Other times, she would tell a story about her mother as if she were still alive, only to quickly correct herself.

At first, a part of me wondered whether she was just tired of showing up for us, or maybe silently protesting my long hours and constant travel. I thought, *Maybe she just wants me to stay home more.* I'd feel a twinge of guilt, wondering if she felt bored or lonely while I was out.

I convinced myself that if I just engaged her more, I could snap her out of it. I cut back on my travel so I could sit with her in the evenings. I'd pull out her word puzzles and try to play them with her, hoping to see that familiar spark return.

I even tried to share the beauty of Tanzania with her, hoping the landscape would stir something within her. I'd take her out to see parts of the country, the vibrant markets, or the coastal views, thinking she just needed a change of scenery. But even as we looked out at the ocean, I could see her drifting. The real heartbreak came when she lost her desire to cook. She had been our chef our entire lives, and suddenly, that came to a screeching halt. When she stopped wanting to go for her daily walks and lost interest in playing her Solitaire, I realized the problem was deeper than anything I could solve with a weekend trip or a puzzle book.

One afternoon, after my mother had gone off on another strange tangent, I called Nancy back in the States. I needed a second opinion, but mostly, I needed someone to tell me I was overreacting.

"Jen, that's not normal," Nancy said, her voice coming through the phone with a clarity that made me flinch.

I shook my head, my "fixer" brain already dismissing the worry. "She's fine, Nancy. I checked her myself."

I had leaned on my years of health training. I checked her

temperature, which was normal. I looked for signs of physical ailment, checked her vitals, and scanned her for any obvious distress. To my eyes, she looked exactly like the woman who had always been my anchor. "Her vitals are perfect," I insisted into the receiver. "Maybe she's just tired, or the heat is getting to her. It can't be that serious."

But Nancy didn't budge. "Call Sandra and see what she thinks," she said. Sandra, our older cousin, was a physician we claimed as our personal doctor whenever an issue arose. Even from across the ocean, Sandra could hear what I was trying to ignore. "No, Jen. It is not normal at all. You need to get her to a doctor," she said.

I agreed reluctantly, mostly to prove I was right. I expected the doctor to tell us she needed more hydration or a new vitamin regimen. Instead, after the tests and the scans, we sat in a quiet office in New York and heard the words that changed everything.

In 2015, we got the official diagnosis: vascular dementia.

Dementia doesn't run in our family; my mom was the only one of seven sisters to have it. The doctor said the mini silent strokes were likely a result of her past habits with alcohol and cigarettes. Even though she had quit years back, they ironically never really left her after all.

As a single mom, my mother had been my lifeline. Because of her, I was able to have such rich professional and personal experiences. She was Anthony's trusted caregiver and my right hand.

Unbeknownst to me, I was entering the "sandwich generation." I found myself holding two worlds at once: a son who was just beginning to find himself and a mother who was slowly losing her way.

The rhythm was changing, but I was still dancing.

Anthony posing with his Force1 camp team in Tanzania.

The family on one of our many flights together.

Chapter Twelve

MUSIC AS A BRIDGE

And I danced.

I went out a lot in those early days. I frequented rooftops in Slipway and Masaki, lounges in Mikocheni and Oysterbay, and beach parties in Mbezi and Kigamboni. We even hosted parties and karaoke nights at the official American community center.

I danced, met people, and soaked up the city. I found my place somewhere between Bongo Flava, Congolese rumba, and the endless loops of Top 40 hits. Luckily, I found a fantastic mix of globetrotting girlfriends who were as happy-go-lucky as I was. When we weren't hosting at home, we explored the vibrant peninsula with its long strip of restaurants and cultural spaces, or went on beach excursions.

Most nights, I served as the designated driver for my friends like Mwikali and Bilen. I wheeled us around in my old Land Rover, a big, loud, blue vehicle that everyone noticed before I even pulled into a parking lot. No creeping was possible with that bad boy.

On weekends, we'd start at one end and wander down, letting the music from each place decide our next stop. Other times, I dabbled in performing my own art. I write poetry mainly as a form of personal release. The poems typically come to me at dramatic moments, such as after heartbreak or extreme disappointment. In Dar, I performed at an event called Poetry Addiction and frequented Soma Books for the Waka Poets sessions with Dada Carol.

After many nights hopping from lounge to club and being around amazing artists like AY, famous for Bongo Flava and hip hop hits. I felt something was missing. I quickly realized I missed the soundtracks of my New York years. I wanted the boom bap, the neo-soul, and the lyricism. I wanted the kind of music that makes you close your eyes, bob your head, and say, "Yass, this is it!"

Of course, I loved the scene and the people in Dar, but I didn't always love the music. Growing up in New York in the 80s and 90s made me a hip hop girl at heart. Given my Caribbean heritage, I also love reggae, R&B, and soul music. I wanted a vibe that blended the soul of home with the spirit of the motherland. Through all my partying and exploring, I realized I wasn't going to find it. If I wanted that feeling again, I'd have to create it.

I remember a specific conversation with Joe and Gaidi. We were out one night, and the DJ was playing the usual set, skipping anything made before 2005.

"You know, I almost never hear the music I love out here."

I voiced my frustration to a few other friends, including old-school Tanzanian rappers like Fid Q and the Masharikanz.

One of them looked at me and shrugged. "I feel you. Why don't we just create our own space?"

A lightbulb went off. That simple question sparked what became The Lounge Tanzania in 2014. Within a week, we were huddled around tables, notebooks in hand, sketching ideas and debating names.

What started as a casual plan for a place to chill with good music quickly grew into a real project. It became a way to bring young people together and provide a platform for their work. As we developed the concept, I kept thinking of the Lyricist Lounge in New York. We adapted that model for Dar es Salaam.

However, we decided to expand the scope beyond hip hop. We wanted to open the stage to a wider range of performers. Tanzania was full of talent, so we invited singers, poets, and comedians to join the mix. Our goal was to create a space specifically for artists to perform and develop their original lyrics.

Our team hit the ground running, posting flyers in venues across town and on social media. Auditions followed quickly, attracting performers from every corner of the city. Some were seasoned pros, and others were brand new, but everyone wanted a shot. Before each show, we huddled wherever we could find space: my living room, local bars, or even half-empty industrial buildings.

The process was intense, screening, rehearsing, and constantly talking through improvements. While only ten people signed up at first, the numbers exploded to twenty-one, then thirty, in just a few weeks. Comedians, poets, singers, and rappers from every genre imaginable came through our doors, all buzzing to share their talent with the growing crowd.

Since we didn't have the cash for a venue, innovation became our best friend. In a perfect world, we would have opened our own spot for total control, but that wasn't going to happen yet. Instead, we scouted for places that were quiet on certain nights and pitched a simple deal: give us the space for free, and we'll bring the crowd.

Club 327 in Mikocheni was the first to say yes. It was run by a husband-and-wife team, Ilona and Lawrence, who remain my friends to this day. Joe's friends Kiche, Ronny, and Agogo from a group called *909* made the introduction. Ilona and Lawrence offered us a Thursday or Friday slot. The setup was exactly what we needed: a small stage, comfortable seating, great lighting, and a quality sound system.

We added spotlights and candles to bring in some color and warmth, and you could feel the electricity in the air.

Our first DJ, Kaka Kahlil, was a friend from California who volunteered his time and equipment, carrying mixers, records, and turntables across the city because he believed in what we were doing. To keep things organized, we held brief auditions before each show, just long enough to see people's potential. We didn't look for perfect acts, just honesty and effort.

The team felt like the perfect mix of dreamers and realists. During auditions, I'd often lean over to Joe and whisper, "Mm, I'm not sure about this one."

Joe would just nudge me back. "Give them a chance, Jen."

If I still wasn't convinced, Shamsa or Gaidi would gently remind me that my opinion wasn't the only one that mattered. Most of the time, they were right. Watching those artists prove me wrong became one of my favorite parts of the process.

One girl in particular still makes me smile. She showed up with the confidence of a young rapper inspired by Lil' Kim: style, swagger, and all the confidence in the world. To me, it felt forced, as if she were pretending to be someone else.

I pulled the team aside and said, "This doesn't fit the Lounge."

They just looked at me, half amused and half fed up. "Jen, relax. This is what young people like."

If they hadn't pushed, she never would have made it past the door. I'm glad they did because the audience loved her. She took over the stage. Meanwhile, I sat in the corner, cringing. But that was the lesson: I didn't have to like everything. It wasn't all about me. The Lounge belonged to the community, and the community always tells you what it needs if you're willing to listen.

I had two firm rules, especially about content: original lyrics and absolutely no cursing. It wasn't about censorship; it was about creating a space where everyone could feel comfortable. The rappers would look at me like, "Seriously?" and I'd just smile: "If your mama wouldn't want to hear it, it's not happening here." We kept to that "family-friendly, original art" rule because it created a space where creativity could thrive while remaining welcoming for everyone.

But then there was this one artist. Well known. Big following. He came from a well-to-do family, had studied in the U.S., and was a master at bilingual rapping. The kind of performer who didn't just walk onstage; he changed the whole mood of the room. The minute he grabbed the mic, the crowd leaned in. His delivery was sharp, his presence effortless, and people hung on every word. You didn't see that kind of command often in Dar, especially among hip hop artists.

Then, right in the middle of his set, he dropped a curse word into his chorus. A loud, vulgar one. The kind that echoed each time he repeated it. I heard it from the back of the crowd and froze mid-step. He was given the same rules as everyone else, but he clearly chose to ignore them. I looked at Joe, who just threw his hands up like, "Don't look at me."

My blood pressure shot straight through the ceiling. We had one rule we repeated so often I could have stitched it onto a banner: clean lyrics only. Original music? Yes. Styles, flavors, confidence? Absolutely. But no cursing. I wanted the Lounge to be a space where anyone could walk in, whether students, aunties, parents, or young folks, without feeling uncomfortable with the content.

When he came offstage, I pulled him aside. I kept my voice even though I was steaming inside.

"What was that?" I asked.

He gave me a slow, smug smile that showed he knew exactly what he'd done. "I know the rules," he said. "But it wouldn't have landed the same without that line."

"Then maybe," I said, "you could have chosen another line."

He shrugged. "Maybe. But I didn't." Then he walked away.

And that was the thing. This was a volunteer show with no contracts, no fines, and no legal consequences. No one was getting paid to perform. He knew he was good and that the crowd liked him. I vowed he would never perform on our stage again, but Gaidi and Joe walked me back from that ledge.

After that night, whenever he graced our stage again, he didn't curse. Not once. Maybe it was respect. Maybe it was the conversation.

Maybe Joe said something to him afterward that got through to him.

Managing the show's lineup was another constant challenge. Nobody wanted the first slot, and if I told an artist they were opening the night, they'd immediately try to negotiate. People often showed up late, forcing us to rearrange the entire schedule on the fly. Joe, our host, saved the day every time. Whenever an artist ran behind, he'd jump onstage to buy us time. Joe had a rare, effortless way of moving between the Tanzanian and expat crowds. He bridged those two worlds seamlessly.

The audience made every stressful moment worthwhile. They came from everywhere, including my colleagues and friends like Ikupa, who was an intern at Africare in DC back in the day, and Babbie, one of Tanzania's most loved on-air personalities who loves reggae more than I do, as well as the performers' families. Our crowd grew into a healthy mix of locals and expats who heard the buzz and wanted to join something different. We saw every race, age, and background together in one warm space. The positive energy was undeniable.

Everyone worked together because we all wanted the project to succeed. Even with power cuts, late arrivals, and technical glitches, we kept going. This was "Bongo" after all. The electricity might fail, or the microphones might pop, but the spirit never broke.

Between acts, our DJs kept the room lively. After DJ Kaka Khalil moved on, we began working with DJ John, a Dar local I met at an Embassy event. They played everything from warm-up tracks to late-night dance beats. We even experimented with music videos, short films, and live art activations, including when the abstract artist from New York, Kool Koor, joined us. These moments transformed The Lounge from a simple event into a true artistic community.

Behind the scenes, money became a real problem after the first couple of years. We needed funding to turn this from a passion project into something sustainable. Sponsorships were our biggest hope and our greatest challenge.

Our shows had grown from a few dozen people to standing-room-only crowds of hundreds. Local papers and blogs began talking about our unique space. With every pitch to beverage companies, banks, or hotels, we pointed to the buzz and the packed rooms. While we received plenty of "no's," we did land small, meaningful contributions, such as raffle vouchers or free drinks for our anniversary shows. It helped, but it wasn't enough.

I often kept myself out of the spotlight during these pitches. I worried that being a foreigner made the deals harder, so I sent Joe or Shamsa instead. They faced the same obstacles. I started to wonder if we weren't "Swahili enough" or simply lacked the right connections. I questioned whether, as an outsider, I was missing the subtle details that would unlock local sponsorships. Whatever the reason, sustainable funding never materialized.

Still, we refused to give up. At first, we didn't charge for entry or pay the artists; it was entirely voluntary. We wanted people to experience the vibe before asking for money. The venues made their profit from the bar.

As the crowds grew, we had to move venues twice to accommodate everyone. Eventually, when we settled at our final spot, Makuti Dar in Oysterbay, we started charging a small fee at the door.

That door money changed things. We finally paid the DJ, who did the heavy lifting of transporting his entire sound system and keeping the energy high all night. We hired Maasai security guards to manage the entrance. Whatever was left went directly to the artists. It wasn't a fortune, but for many of them, it was the first time they had ever been paid for their art. That meant everything to them and to me.

The Lounge was more than a monthly event. It truly made a difference in the arts and entertainment scene. After many late nights and a lot of effort, it became a place where artists like Mex Cortez, inspired by legendary artists like Hashim Dogo, found their voices and grew their fanbase. Chi, a singer, was inspired by what we started and went on to create her own series focused on vocalists. We faced sleepless nights, technical issues, and struggled to find sponsors, but seeing artists go from performing at The Lounge to headlining their own shows made me proud. Watching them grow showed what our space made possible and that it was all worth it in the end.

None of this would have happened without the great team and supporters behind it. They were passionate and gave their time and energy because they believed in the idea as much as I did. In addition to the people I've already mentioned, others helped us tremendously along the way, including Kibacha, Samra, and Msia. For our anniversary, the incomparable comedian and host extraordinaire, Evans Bukuku, would share the stage with Joe as our special co-host. We also had guest acts as part of our show when they came to town, such as Akua Naru, Lah Tere, and Maya Wegerif (also known as Shomadjozi). Locally, we were able to get the likes of Fid Q, Damian Soul, Mad Ice, and Grace Matata to elevate our stage from time to time.

Even after I left Tanzania in 2017, the show kept going. My co-host Joe, a legend in his own right, and Shamsa, our resident literary artist, who helped at the door and shone on stage, kept it going for a couple of years. It was no longer just my passion project; it became something valuable to the whole community.

One moment that still makes me smile is when Anthony, about twelve, bravely stepped onto the stage during one of our shows. He recited a poem about basketball, maybe about Michael Jordan, that he had written at school.

I remembered the hours we spent rehearsing, his nerves before he went onstage, and how he stumbled over his lines, anxious and unsure. Sometimes he forgot a line and looked to me for reassurance. But when it was his turn, he stood tall under the lights, shoulders squared, just as he had practiced in the bathroom mirror while brushing his teeth. He tapped the mic once.

"This is for anyone who thought sports was the only way out," he said, his voice cracking but holding steady.

Then he performed three rhyming stanzas about shooting hoops, algebra, and how unfair bedtime was. The crowd laughed at the punchline and clapped along to the beat we had practiced the night before. I stood on the side and felt a burst of pride for Anthony, my baby, standing under the lights and sharing his words with new confidence.

My mom was there with us that night, watching him too. I could see the pride in her eyes as well.

When he finished, he glanced over, found my eyes, and gave me his gap-toothed grin that mirrored mine.

Joe cued the next act, but I stayed where I was, watching Anthony hop down from the stage and rush over to me, excited.

He handed me the mic as if it were a relay baton. "Your turn, Mom," he whispered, his breath smelling of the mint gum he'd begged for earlier.

I took it, my throat tight, and realized he wasn't just giving me equipment. He was passing me the next part of a race that now belonged to both of us. My mom promptly came over to us and told him it was time to go home. Our taxi driver was waiting for them outside.

As I came back from walking them out, I caught my reflection in the cracked mirror behind the bar: same eyes, but a new horizon. The little girl from Queens who once whispered wishes into the dark was now watching her son take the stage she built from borrowed speakers and a hope that defied the horizon. The circle hadn't just closed; it had grown large enough for both of us to stand inside.

The Lounge Tanzania's legacy lives far beyond the nights we curated in Dar es Salaam and, later, in Moshi. It became a blueprint for what happens when community, creativity, and intention collide. What started as my search for the sound and soul I missed from my New York days grew into a cultural home where artists felt seen, where young talent found its voice, and where a new standard of artistry and excellence quietly took root in the city.

The Lounge didn't just entertain; it nurtured talent, forged lifelong bonds, and proved that when you create a space rooted in authenticity and love, people rise to meet it. Even years later, former attendees and artists still speak about how it shaped their confidence, their craft, and their belief that world-class art could be made right where they stood, no passport required.

When COVID hit, we had to stop live shows. We tried moving online, but it just wasn't the same. In addition to our online presence, we documented some of the best performers at our show through a mixtape called "The Lounge Tanzania Mixtape Vol. 1" in 2020. I co-produced it with friends at 41 Records Studio in Dar, and Stone Town Records in Zanzibar. It features 17 tracks in both Swahili and English, including a poem by yours truly.

Years later, people still ask me, "What made The Lounge special?"

For me, the answer is simple.

We weren't building an organization. We were building a pulse. It was a living, breathing entity, vibrant with the energy from every note played and every soul present. It was a platform we built with our own hands, our time, and our stubborn love for music and lyrics. It was the bridge between our work and our joy, uniting stress and escape. It was a place where music, young people, and those young at heart, and purpose came together, allowing everyone to dream big without apology. Everyone cared enough to show up, debate, laugh, dream, and stay up late, even if they had work the next morning. Even now, people tell me they wish the Lounge would come back. Honestly, I feel the same way.

As I prepared to leave Tanzania, I realized that the spirit of the Lounge wasn't tied to a specific room or a set of speakers. It was something I carried within me, a pulse that seemed to expand and pick up new rhythms with every new destination.

Every time I accepted a new post, the ritual was the same: I packed my bags, telling myself I was going to serve, help, and leave the place better than I found it. That was the plan. But somewhere along the way, each country quietly changed the script. Tanzania did it best of all. I arrived thinking I had answers to give, experiences to share, lessons to teach. Instead, I left heavier with gifts I never listed.

I thought I was the one doing the giving. Turns out, the giving went both ways, and I was the one who came out richer, kinder, and a little more whole than when I stepped off the plane.

Tanzania was, and still is, my favorite posting. The music in the air, the shows we put together, the community, and Zanzibar. All of it made my time there richer and gave me lifelong friends I now call family. I loved it so much that I asked for a one-year extension so Anthony could finish middle school there. For once, the bureaucracy said yes.

Still, at the end of the day, leaving hurt more than I can explain. Dar wasn't just a city to me. It was a whole small universe where I found my people. Saying goodbye felt like peeling off a layer of skin I had grown to like.

Of course, I had to leave "Mr. Cool" behind, too. After a while, we realized we were not cut from the same cloth. My departure provided the perfect backdrop for our separation. Neither of us wanted a long-distance relationship. He wasn't going to leave his daughter to follow me, and I certainly wasn't going to alter my trajectory to stay for him in Tanzania.

The farewells began weeks early: lunches, dinners, all-white parties, yacht cruises, and the final Lounge show that turned into a full-blown send-off. Artists sang songs they had written for us. Someone handed me a giant painting of me laughing with my friends. I cried so hard I probably watered the floor. There was cake, champagne, and too many hugs.

Joe, who had become like my little brother by then, closed the night with a song he wrote just for me. That's when I really lost it. It was so emotional and beautiful. Anthony and I still borrow the hook whenever we miss someone: "hi again, bye again." We use it for old friends. We say it about Mom even to this day. It's our little thing now.

We taped the last of the boxes and sold the big blue Land Rover to an incoming officer. We took the usual summer flight home, but this time, August wouldn't bring us back.

Looking back, I can say that Tanzania gave me a whole life, not just a job. It taught me how to handle heavy work, both in the office and at home, and still dance when the music played. It was a place where I could be serious and silly, driven and free. It showed me that community is oxygen and that joy is a form of resistance.

Some moments still shine brighter than the rest: shaking Jane Goodall's hand at a work event or standing in a crowd on the Embassy grounds while President Obama talked about Africa's future. Then there was watching Anthony bounce the ball, shoot, and make 3-pointers as if he'd been born for it. Those were huge. But the real magic lived in ordinary nights: chai that never got cold, with chapati and samosas, while we talked about everything. Karaoke and rooftop dancing, laughter so loud it drowned out the ocean.

When it was time to go, I didn't just leave with boxes or a *Tinga Tinga* name board. I left with a clearer heart and a new way of being. The friendships, the music, the laughter, and even the heartbreaks.

Tanzania gave me joy that didn't need permission. It gave me the majestic Indian Ocean. It gave me the woman I am now: someone who knows exactly what she will and will not carry. Tanzania is the gift that keeps on giving. It showed me so much love, and I'm eternally grateful.

Hi again, bye again, Tanzania. *Nakupenda sana.*

Celebrating an anniversary show with the Lounge Tanzania crew members Joe, Shamsa, and Gaidi.

Zanzibar vacation with Nancy and Stephanie.

Enjoying a night out with the Dar es Salaam ladies' crew.

Celebrating at my all-white farewell party on a yacht in Tanzania.

Chapter Thirteen

THE VIEW FROM THE RIDGE

"Ms. Jennifer. She hasn't moved all day."

Sharon, the woman I'd hired to help us settle into our house in Pretoria, stood in the kitchen doorway. Her face carried a mix of worry and confusion. I followed her eyes into the living room and felt my stomach drop.

My mother was sitting exactly where I had left her that morning. She stared at a blank patch of wall, her hands folded in her lap, as if someone had pressed pause.

"Mom?" I walked over, keeping my voice gentle. "You've got to move around a little, okay?"

Nothing. She did not blink. When I looked closer, I realized no one was home. She was somewhere else entirely.

In Tanzania, I had brushed aside moments like this. When she stopped cooking or lost interest in the things she loved, like her Word Find puzzles, I told myself she was bored. Worse, I sometimes thought she was being stubborn.

I couldn't have been more wrong.

Dementia is not only about misplaced keys. It is a thief that sneaks in and rewires a person until they become a stranger in their own body.

Looking at her like that, I felt sad and scared at the same time.

This was different from any other challenge I faced with my mom. This was a quiet, hollowed version of the woman who raised me. There was no feistiness, no push back. I didn't understand it all at the time. How does one fix a brain that is slowly erasing itself? How do you fight something that is not an attack?

Seeing her like that, vacant and unreachable, hit me in such a different way. My brain didn't know how to process that kind of grief, especially when it was tangled up in so much confusion. She was still sitting right in front of me, but the mother I knew had already started leaving the building.

I couldn't fall apart in front of Sharon, and there was no way I could let Anthony see me break down. So, I did what I knew how to do. I went up to my bedroom, locked the door, and lay on my bed. I cried for the woman who once filled our house with good-smelling food and songs, and for the quiet stranger now sitting in my living room. I gave myself five minutes. Then I stood up, put on my superwoman mask, and went back downstairs.

Being back in South Africa felt almost poetic. Eighteen years earlier, I had arrived as a twenty-six-year-old Peace Corps volunteer, stepping off a rattling pickup truck in rural Limpopo. Now the three of us, Anthony, my mother, and I, had landed in Pretoria to build a home in yet another country. The Agency placed us in an affluent, peaceful neighborhood called Waterkloof Ridge. Our small compound was lovely, though the driveway was so steep it felt more like a dare than a road.

Uber drivers would stop at the top, look down, and text me, "Ma'am, my brakes aren't that brave." I would begrudgingly have to make the long trek up. Friends tried it once, then very politely suggested that we meet at a nearby restaurant next time.

If you survived the descent, though, the view was worth it.

Sharon, and later Judith, quickly became our saving grace. As my mother's mind began to slip and Anthony struggled through high school with ADHD, I couldn't be everywhere at once. Both ladies became the steady heartbeat of the house while I was out trying to hold the rest of the world together.

Sharon and Judith, were truly the quiet anchors of our household. Both from Zimbabwe, they brought not only skill and dedication to everything they did with cleaning, cooking, running errands, and keeping the household moving, but also a warmth and reliability that made daily life feel lighter and more grounded. I trusted them completely and felt wholly at ease with them in our space; in time, they stopped feeling like staff and simply became part of the family. What I cherished most was our shared Zimbabwe connection. We easily shared meaningful conversations about Zim, about politics and current events, about life back across the border, woven into ordinary days in Pretoria. Their presence was a gift, and their care, constancy, and kindness left a lasting imprint on that chapter of my life.

At work, the mission was its own mountain. I was officially posted in Pretoria, but my job covered parts of southern Africa. I was a Regional Health Officer for one of USAID's largest missions, responsible for health programs across several countries.

Most weeks, I was moving between airports and ministry offices: Maseru, Mbabane, Windhoek, Gaborone, Luanda. About twenty percent of my year was spent on planes. Thank goodness for the rockstars on my team, like Tovho and Thembeka, who helped keep me on track. I did so many same-day trips that I'd land, change shoes in the airport bathroom, head straight into a meeting, and act like this was completely normal.

After a while, it was.

One country from that regional role stood out to me more than the others. Lesotho. The first time I landed in Maseru, I was completely stunned.

From the plane window, the tiny kingdom looked unreal. Wide open grasslands stretched out in every direction, brushed in soft gold and green. Mountains rose sharply from the land, layer after layer, dramatic and clean, as if placed there on purpose. Even driving out of the airport, I remember thinking, *This might be one of the most beautiful places I've ever seen.*

Lesotho earns its nickname, the Kingdom in the Sky. The air is thin and crisp, the light so sharp it feels like it could cut glass, and the peaks sit so close you almost expect to reach out and touch one. It's picture-perfect.

But it didn't take long to understand the other side of that beauty.

Those same mountains that stopped me in my tracks were daily obstacles for the people who lived there. Roads were steep, narrow, and often impassible. Villages sat tucked into hillsides that looked peaceful from a distance and punishing up close. What felt like a scenic drive to me could mean a full day or more of frustrating travel for someone else.

Beauty, in Lesotho, came with a cost.

In healthcare, the cost was clearest. Delivering medicine was not just a matter of logistics; it was a test of physical endurance. Motorbike riders in bright yellow vests wound up narrow dirt paths to reach shepherds whose homes were days from the nearest clinic. Community health workers crossed rivers sometimes on foot, timing their steps carefully since there were no bridges or safety gear. Someone on the far side was waiting for life-saving drugs.

For visitors, the mountains and rivers were the draw. For locals, they were obstacles to cross again and again just to survive. Many faced long, difficult journeys switching between walking, rickety public taxis that were few and far between, or riding donkeys. What should have been a simple trip to the clinic often meant a full-day trek over freezing ridges or across swollen rivers. When your life depended on medicine taken every day, the very landscape became the enemy.

Lesotho carried staggering health burdens. One in four adults lived with HIV. Whole generations had been lost, leaving grandmothers to raise grandchildren who should have had parents.

We supported a wide range of programs, including treatment scale-up (the push to get everyone diagnosed onto effective HIV treatment), prevention for adolescent girls, male circumcision services, supply chains, and data systems to track those left behind.

In the few years I was there, I saw progress. Lesotho was moving toward epidemic control faster than anyone had predicted.

While I never had to cross any rivers myself, those missions across the region became my lifeblood. I wanted to make sure we reached every person possible, delivering life-saving services to as many as we could. We kept programs like DREAMS for girls going strong because prevention and empowerment were as important as treatment. This wasn't just running a program. It was finishing what that bright-eyed Peace Corps girl had started eighteen years earlier.

But the deeper I went into the work, the more the past started to catch up with me.

South Africa held more than just my career. It held the ghosts of the young woman I used to be. This was the country where I had met Al, Anthony's father, and knowing he was still out there somewhere in the United States, unhoused and unreachable, was a reality I couldn't quite wrap my head around or forget.

One afternoon, while I was unpacking a box in Pretoria, a faded photo slipped out. It was from our engagement party in Limpopo back in 2001. There I was in my twenties, glowing in a royal blue outfit, with Al beside me grinning like he'd won the lottery.

Anthony walked in, spotted the picture, and went quiet. He leaned over and rested his chin on my shoulder, looking from the man in the photo to his own reflection. It hit me hard then. I had brought my son back to the place that made him, and now I owed him the rest of his story.

We headed north to Limpopo. I wanted Anthony to meet his father's family, and I needed to face the place where I'd first set foot in South Africa almost two decades earlier. As I gripped the wheel of my red sedan, my nerves were a mess. I worried about old resentments and unspoken wounds, but my fears didn't matter as much as Anthony's right to see the people who shared his bloodline. He deserved to know where he came from. I also wanted him to see where I spent my Peace Corps days.

When we reached my ex-in-law's house, the veranda came alive. Aunts, uncles, and cousins spilled out as if a film paused in 2001 had suddenly started playing again. Al's mom, Anthony's Gogo, took one look at him, tall and lanky in his basketball slides, and opened her arms so wide, wrapping around him like a gift. She held him until he finally laughed and hugged her back.

Inside, the welcome was a whirlwind. Cold Coca Cola and Fanta appeared instantly, and one of the kids was sent to the spaza shop to get some snacks before I could even protest. They brought out old photo albums, and Anthony sat quietly, tracing his father's face with one finger. When he finally looked up and smiled, it was that same tilted, mischievous grin I remembered from years ago. The whole family erupted in cheers.

Eventually, the talk turned to the shadow in the room: Al. Where was he?

By now, they knew we were divorced. I told them the rest of the truth as gently as I could. He was experiencing homelessness, and my efforts to bring him back to South Africa had failed. I handed over the private investigator's contact information and a clear way for them to get help to find him.

"I tried," I said.

They nodded and took the number. They promised they would follow up, but I don't know if they did. Some burdens are just too heavy to pick up.

We finished our cold drinks and hugged goodbye. Anthony and I went on to visit several other families from my Peace Corps days, and I pointed out the schools I used to work at along the way. That evening, we went back and stayed with the Thlako family, sleeping in the same house where I first met Al. After dinner, we sat around watching local soapies like old times.

I turned to my host mom and said to her, "You know this is all your fault. You're the one who hooked me up with Al in the first place."

She looked at me and said "Sho" with a big grin, and we both started to laugh heartily. A real full circle moment.

As we drove away from Limpopo the next afternoon, the trip didn't feel like a waste. Anthony had been given something no government system and no absent father could take away. He had an afternoon surrounded by people who instantly loved him. I had given him the other half of his story. Contact information was exchanged. What he chose to do with it was up to him.

Back in Pretoria, nothing had paused while we were gone. My mother kept forgetting. Each week, it took her a little more effort to recall where she was or why. Anthony returned to school, and I went back to work.

The mission moved forward, and so did I. At least on the surface.

I was functioning, but I wasn't well. Amid all that motion, a pain had settled into my left hip. It had lingered for months, easy to ignore, easy to push through. I blamed stress, constant travel, too many hours on planes, and too many years of refusing to slow down. I also knew it was partly genetic. My mom had osteoarthritis, and by that time, a few of my aunts had undergone all kinds of replacement surgeries.

One morning, I tried to stand from the couch, and the pain struck like a fist of fire. I crumpled back down, gasping. The hip that had whispered complaints for months was now screaming.

It had started gradually. By the end of Tanzania, I was limping regularly. I tried to hide it. At one of our Lounge shows, a singer pulled me aside and asked if I was okay. He'd noticed the limp. I laughed it off, blamed age, swallowed another ibuprofen, and kept going.

When I arrived in Pretoria, the pain was no longer something I could work around.

One day, I called in sick, something I rarely did, and limped to an orthopedic clinic the next day.

The surgeon slid the MRI films onto the light box and went quiet.

"Jennifer," he said finally, "this isn't normal wear and tear."

He pointed to the joint: bone-on-bone arthritis, yes. Then he traced faint white lines threading through the socket and femoral neck.

"Microfractures," he said. "Old ones. Healed badly. When were you in the accident?"

I stared at him. "What accident?"

In that moment, two crashes I hadn't thought about in years came rushing back. The first was in 1999 during my Peace Corps days; the second happened later, while I was still in South Africa. I never imagined those moments were just waiting, ready to find me decades later.

Those old impacts, layered onto genetics, years of travel, long days on my feet, heavy bags, and a body that rarely stopped, had quietly eroded the cartilage.

The surgeon recommended total hip replacement. I scheduled it in November 2017.

The night before, I lay awake in my private hospital room in Pretoria, listening to the hum of machines and muffled voices in the corridor. My mind ran through practical lists. Permission slips. School lunches. Who would remind Mom to eat if I didn't come back?

I was a single parent. My own mother was already slipping away. If something happened to me, Anthony would be left alone. That weight pressed on my chest as they wheeled me into the operating room. Luckily, Sharon had agreed to sleep in with us during this time to help keep the house in order.

When I woke, my body felt foreign, heavy, rearranged. The

pain was sharp, but underneath it ran relief. I was still here. I opened my eyes, and tears of joy immediately filled them when I saw Mom, Anthony, and Joe at my bedside. Joe came all the way from Tanzania to help with my recovery. What a Godsend.

I spent five days in the hospital relearning the basics: how to stand, go up and down stairs, and trust my leg. Then they sent me home with neon green crutches, a stack of instructions, pain pills, and a calendar built entirely around recovery.

Physical therapists came to the house and guided me through each careful step. Simple things turned into negotiations, getting out of bed, showering, and getting dressed. I couldn't drive. I hated the dependence, hated it more because I didn't want to be a burden.

After a couple of months, I returned to work on crutches, moving slowly through meetings. Gradually, the pain eased. Strength came back. The limp faded and then vanished. It felt like a miracle.

The surgery was a resounding success. To this day, my left hip gives me no trouble. It holds me up without complaint, a quiet piece of titanium doing what flesh and bone could no longer manage.

For the first time in years, I wasn't moving through a fog of physical pain. I felt like a machine that had finally been oiled, ready to tackle the mounting pressure at the office. I threw myself back into the mission with a vengeance. I figured if my body could be put back together with metal and grit, surely I could do the same for our regional strategy. I spent my days sprinting from the tarmac to ministry hallways, as usual, obsessed with reaching those final targets in Lesotho and starting up new programs in Angola.

But while I was gaining ground at work, I was losing it at home.

I had fixed my hip, and I had connected Anthony to his roots, but the one thing I couldn't manage was the steady decline of my mother. While I was in Botswana negotiating contracts, she was drifting further into the gray. The stillness Sharon had noticed months earlier was now punctuated by moments of total confusion.

I realized then that the most unbreakable thing I had to do wasn't walking after surgery. It was admitting that I couldn't be a

179

regional health officer and a full-time caregiver to two dependents at the same time.

To keep Mom safe and me sane, I had to send her back home. By winter 2018, the decision was made: she had to return to Maryland.

The plan sounded simple enough on paper. Nancy and I discussed how we would fly her back, settle her near her doctor, and find a senior apartment where someone could check on her every day. We figured she just needed closer medical attention and a little bit of oversight. But before we committed to a facility, we wanted to give her a softer landing. We thought it would be better for her to stay with a friend or a relative first to ease her back into life in the States.

Then came the question no one wanted to answer: Whose home would actually take her in?

I called Miss Lorraine, Mom's closest friend. She was really more like a younger sister. They had raised their kids together and shared recipes, gossip, and grief. She was family in every way except by name. I thought she would say yes before I even finished the sentence.

She didn't.

A few days later, she called me back. Her voice was soft and almost apologetic. "Jennifer, I talked to my husband. We just can't. The kids, the stairs, the dogs. It is too much."

There was a long pause on the line.

"We can help look for an apartment, though," she added.

I felt the phone grow heavy in my hand. I felt angry, empty, and afraid. But what hurt most wasn't the "no." It was who said it.

Miss Lorraine had once stood on my mother's doorstep in Maryland with two toddlers, a suitcase, and two nervous dogs after her husband put her out in the middle of the night. Twice. Mom didn't ask a single question. She opened the door, took the dogs, let them share her room, and kept them for months. She paid the light bills and drove Lorraine to work.

Now, decades later, Miss Lorraine stood in the house my mother had helped her keep and said, "My husband says we can't."

The same man who once put her out was now the reason she couldn't open her door for my mother. The man Mom had fed and prayed for was now the one deciding Mom didn't belong.

The phone felt like lead as I hung up. Across the room, my mother was folding the same sweater for the twentieth time, humming a Haitian lullaby she no longer truly remembered.

A promise escaped my lips, breaking the silence of the quiet room. "I will make sure you are well taken care of, Mom. You are safe with me."

I became the daughter who would never let anyone say there wasn't room for the woman who always made room.

That promise quickly turned into logistics. Plane tickets. Medical records. Suitcases stacked against the walls.

I spent weeks packing up a life that was slowly coming apart. I told myself I was giving her a soft landing in Maryland, something safe and dignified. But most days, I packed with tears slipping down my face. I folded her clothes, wrapped things she had loved, and realized she had no idea what any of it meant anymore. She did not know what we were saving. She did not know what we were leaving behind.

The hardest part was the notes.

I wrote them carefully, in clear handwriting, like instructions for a child. Her name. My phone number. Nancy's phone number and address. A sentence I never imagined I would have to write about my own mother: *I have dementia. Please help me.*

I slipped the notes into her purse. Tucked one into her coat pocket. Checked and rechecked, the way I used to double-lock doors. Each note felt like a small surrender. Another line crossed that I could not uncross.

I had spent years making hard decisions at work. I managed budgets, teams, and crises across countries. None of that prepared me for writing instructions meant to protect my mother from herself.

On December 29, 2018, Anthony and I stood at O.R. Tambo International Airport and watched my mother be escorted in a wheelchair toward the gate.

We stayed still until she disappeared.

I had done everything "by the book." I'd spoken to the airline agents personally to ensure her dementia was noted. I'd requested the wheelchair and the meet-and-greet and emphasized that, while she was still mobile, she needed a watchful eye. I was told Flight 207 was a simple "technical stop" in Dakar for fuel. No one gets off, they assured me.

Nancy called at 11:00 a.m. Pretoria time the next morning. Her voice wasn't just anxious; it was hollow. "Jen, the plane landed at Dulles twenty minutes ago. Mom isn't on it."

The world went silent. A cold, sharp dread took over.

I immediately called the airline's Operations Manager in Dakar, who had thankfully called Nancy and shared his call-back number. His voice was calm, which only made me feel more frantic.

"Ma'am, there was an oversight," he said. "The crew missed the notes on the travel record. Your mother deplaned with the passengers, ending her journey here. We didn't realize she was missing until the aircraft was already back in the air, halfway across the Atlantic."

I pictured my mother, disoriented and confused, standing in the heat of a Senegalese terminal while wondering why Nancy wasn't there to hug her.

"She has dementia," my voice was shaking. "She has daily medication she can't take alone. She needs supervision. You left her in a strange country."

Then came the blow that nearly leveled me. The manager told me the next flight to Washington wouldn't stop in Dakar for three and a half days due to the New Year's holiday. He suggested putting her in a hotel until Wednesday. Three and a half days.

To a woman who couldn't remember what city she was in, three days was an eternity. It felt like a death sentence for her peace of mind. I hung up and went into "Director mode" because it was the only way I knew how to survive the panic. I was in South Africa, Nancy was in Maryland, and our mother was lost in Senegal. I called the U.S. Embassy in Dakar's emergency line.

"Hi John, my name is Jennifer Erie with USAID/Southern Africa," I said, my voice finally cracking. "My mother is lost in your airport. I need your help, please."

While the Embassy team scrambled, I realized one small detail that might save her. Mom's first language was French. In the middle of this nightmare, she had landed in a place where she could at least speak her heart.

The Embassy duty officer found her and called me from the terminal. When he put her on the phone, her voice sounded soft and innocent. "Jennifer? I don't know where I am, Cherie, but the people here are very nice. They speak my language." He then took her to the nearest hotel, where, by the grace of God, one of my USAID colleagues, Laura, met her and ensured she was checked in properly.

I wept. I am not sure if it was from relief or guilt. Probably both. In the meantime, I was also negotiating with the airline to have her put on another earlier flight while searching on my laptop to see whether Nancy or I could get out sooner to pick her up personally.

The airline refused to put her on a partner flight, calling it a customer service issue. I didn't care about their policies anymore. With the help of a local travel agent, the Embassy found, I spent an additional couple of thousand dollars on a one-way seat on another airline that same evening. I didn't think twice about the money.

Nancy met her at Dulles the next day. When Mom walked through the gate, she was cheerful, as if she'd just had a long layover in a pleasant café. "Hi, Cherie," she said to Nancy. "Are you picking me up from the airport?"

Nancy hugged her tight and then cried silently the whole way to the car. I sat on my couch in Pretoria and finally released a breath I had been holding for twenty-four hours. We had come so close to a total disaster.

Nancy became the anchor for the next chapter of Mom's life. We moved her into a little senior apartment in Prince George's County in early 2019. It was a two-bedroom with pale yellow walls and a bay window that looked out on a parking lot and a strip of trees. Nancy found the place, and Barbara, a soft-spoken woman who came in to help.

For a while, it actually worked.

Then the messages started.

Barbara: She didn't touch the chicken I left.

Nancy, 7:00 p.m.: The plate is still on the counter. Exactly where Barbara put it.

The building manager: Miss Ginette was in the lobby in her nightgown asking for the bus to Haiti. We walked her back upstairs.

Every message landed like a stone in my chest. No matter how many miles were between us, that helplessness sat right there in the room with me.

I was in Namibia when Nancy called me, her voice full of worry.

"She isn't showering, Jen," she said. "Barbara says she just changes her clothes and insists she already bathed."

I felt the old anger rise, not just at the disease or the distance, but at myself for ever believing that four hours of caregiving a day would be enough.

We added hours, then more. Eventually, we brought in a second caregiver just for the evenings, but I was starting to realize that no amount of patchwork scheduling could keep her safe anymore. Plus, we couldn't afford it anymore.

Finding a full-time home became its own mission, one that was quieter and much harder than any project I had ever run at the office. We finally moved her into a specialized care facility in February 2020.

As I watched the paperwork get filed, I made a quiet, fierce promise to myself. Distance would not be allowed to turn into abandonment. I was a woman who lived on airplanes, and I decided then that I would cross that ocean as often as I needed to. If it meant every single one of my leave days was spent in a chair in Maryland, so be it.

I would sit beside her bed and hold the hand that had once held mine. I didn't care about vacations or rest. I only cared about being there.

I actually looked forward to the moments that used to frustrate me. I was ready to sit with her at 7:30 a.m. and have the same old argument over how much sugar belonged in her Cap'n Crunch cereal. I was ready to be the one to guide her into the shower, moving slowly and carefully so she never felt small or lost her dignity. I wanted to be the one to answer the same question ten times and, on the eleventh, choose patience.

If she needed to hear that we were going back to Haiti tomorrow, I would tell her exactly that. I would look into her eyes and promise her the mother she had lost forty years ago, just to see her smile.

I walked out of that facility believing I had this handled. I had the resources. I had the will. I had a flight schedule.

I didn't know that while I was making my plans, the world was already beginning to close with very different plans of its own.

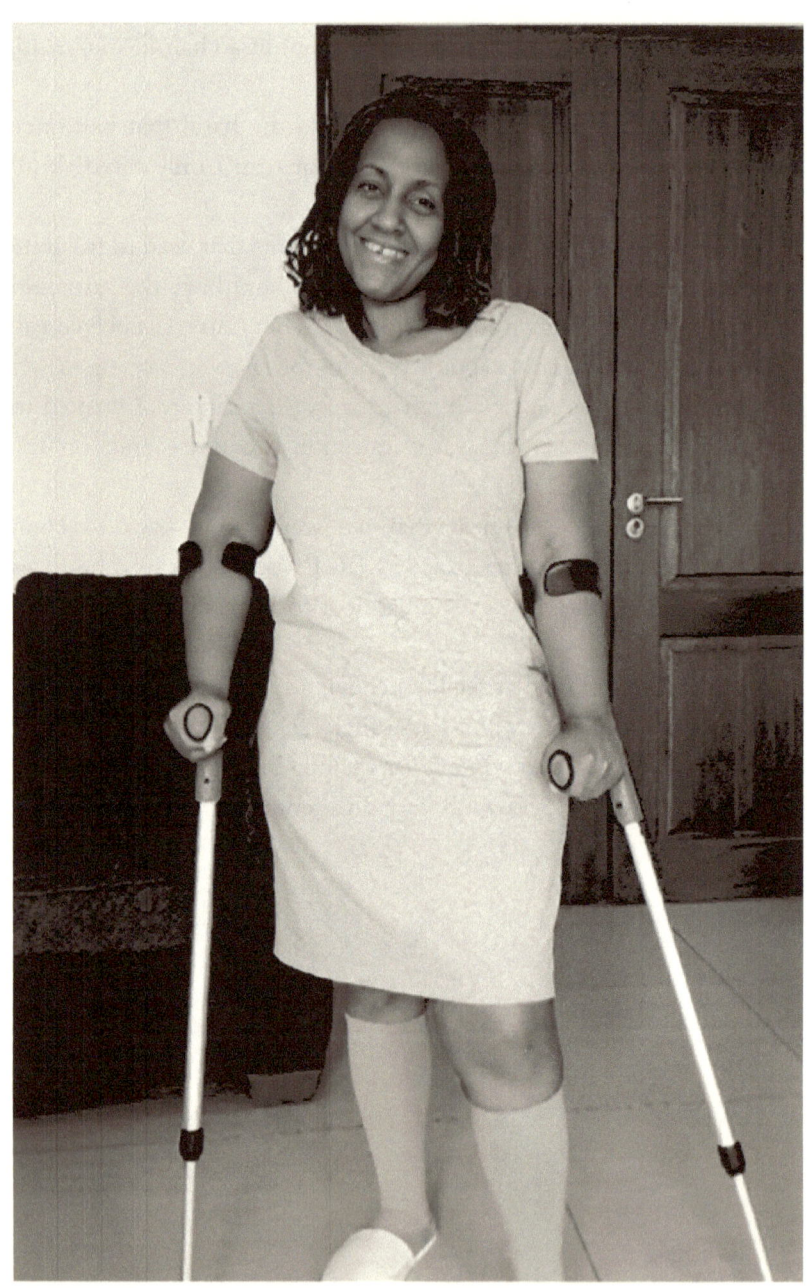

Navigating Pretoria on crutches following my hip surgery in November 2017.

Chapter Fourteen

GROUNDED

We were the last two passengers still grinning at our gate in the Julius Nyerere International Airport. The afterglow of the Lounge's sixth anniversary hadn't worn off. All those years of hauling speakers and coaching eager rappers from the streets of Dar onto our stage had led to this: a roaring, hip hop-infused sing-along. My ears were still ringing with the final bars of the headliner's set, a young man who had started at our open mic as a first-timer and ended the night as a star.

While everyone else in the departures hall flipped into travel-stress mode, Anthony and I were still floating. We had our boarding passes in hand, certain the music could carry us all the way back home to Pretoria. That music had helped us build a sanctuary for poets and rappers, a place that felt untouchable. But even as the bass still hummed in my bones, my mind performed its habitual three-way split.

First, I was the Founder, still savoring the victory of our sixth anniversary, proving our community could thrive. Then, I was the Remote Caregiver, my thoughts drifting across the Atlantic to Maryland. I mentally checked the time there, wondering if Mom was settling into her new care facility or if she was currently standing at a nurse's station, demanding a bus ticket back to Haiti. Finally, I was the Officer-in-Charge, mentally opening my laptop to a calendar that was a battlefield of high-stakes missions. I was tasked with responsibly pivoting millions in PEPFAR funding to local partners in Botswana, Lesotho, and Namibia.

I had meetings lined up to finalize landscape analyses and risk management plans that would move Lesotho from zero local funding to a significant thirty percent. I had to be on the ground to lead the interviews, look those twenty-five local organizations in the eye, and facilitate the panels that would finally give them a seat at the table. It was the 'journey to self-reliance' we had preached for years, and it was finally happening. My goal was to reach Pretoria, sign the awards, and drive that momentum forward.

I also needed to check in with our new housekeeper, Judith who had recently started with us after Sharon moved on to new adventures. Anthony kept patting his hoodie pocket, checking for his phone. Normally, he'd be lost in Snapchat or playing video games, but tonight the screen stayed locked on one photo: Snoopy, our scrappy four-pound mini Yorkie we'd brought home a year ago. That dog had wrapped himself around Anthony's heart from day one and hadn't let go.

"Do you think Judith remembered to refresh his water?" he asked for the fourth time.

I flicked my boarding pass against his forehead. "Relax. Judith's handled bigger crises than a thirsty puppy."

"But he only drinks from the left bowl…"

The kid who used to forget his own homework now kept a running checklist for a creature that chewed left sneakers and demanded bottled spring water. Somewhere along the way, he'd turned into Snoopy's fiercely devoted dad.

I put my arm around him, feeling the bony shoulder that used to end at my waist. "Look, even if Judith gives him tap water instead of the bottled spring water you insist on, Snoopy will survive. He's a dog, Anthony, not a sommelier."

"A what?"

I opened my mouth to explain, but the speakers cut me off.

"Final call, South African Airways SA190 to Johannesburg. All remaining passengers to Gate 4."

The vocabulary lesson could wait. Home and Snoopy were calling. We stepped forward, shoes squeaking on the shiny floor, boarding passes raised like victory flags.

Then the microphone crackled. It wasn't the crisp, automated accent we'd heard all day, but a local gate agent whose voice tipped toward terror.

"Attention, please. SA190 is grounded. Technical circumstances."

The hall seemed to freeze. Every departure screen flickered, then bled red: DELAYED. CANCELLED.

What followed was pure, unscripted chaos.

Even with all my years hopping continents, missed connections, red-eye layovers, flights canceled for everything from volcanic ash to civil unrest, I'd never seen a departure hall fracture like this.

Twenty accents collided in one roaring wave of disbelief. The German backpackers ahead of us unleashed a multilingual string of curses. A tour guide screamed into two phones at once.

Overhead, the loudspeaker looped its calm, robotic apology: *We regret any inconvenience this may have caused.*

I scanned the mess, caught Anthony's eye, and nodded toward a row of plastic seats. It was only then that I noticed a Ministry of Health pull-up banner nearby warning of COVID-19 signs and symptoms. No answers were coming from that desperate surge at the agent's counter. I dialed Joe and told him to circle back. We clearly weren't getting out tonight.

By the time we made it back to the hotel, the options were grim. We spent the night glued to phones and laptops, refreshing airline sites, begging agents for anything headed south. By some small miracle, we snagged two seats on a flight the next afternoon.

We touched down at OR Tambo late Sunday, exhausted but intact. Anthony dropped his bags in the hallway and made a beeline for Snoopy, who launched himself at the boy like he'd been sprung from prison. For a few hours, with the little dog yapping and turning circles around Anthony's legs, the world felt normal again.

But by Monday night, "normal" was gone.

I sat on the sofa that Monday night, laptop on my knees, TV murmuring, phone buzzing like it had a pulse of its own. We'd heard about the "Wuhan virus" back in January, but we filed it under "someone else's problem." In the office, we'd see it mentioned by colleagues in Asia, but didn't pay close enough attention: a China issue, something that would fizzle out long before it reached the southern tip of Africa.

Then, just like that, early March brought the first case to South African soil. Briefings flipped from "if" to "when." Now, the "when" had arrived.

The national anthem cut through the room. I looked up, momentarily annoyed at the interruption, then froze. President Ramaphosa filled the screen, face grim.

"My fellow South Africans..."

I lowered my phone and sat up straighter.

He started talking about COVID-19. About numbers. About staying home. I remember thinking, *This wasn't a drill. This is serious.* Then he said it.

"Nationwide lockdown."

I nearly jumped out of the couch.

"Wait, what?!" I said out loud, to no one.

He kept going. Twenty-one days. Starting at midnight on Thursday. No movement. Only medical emergency exceptions.

As he laid out the rules, the notification every diplomat dreads flashed across my laptop: Authorized Departure, Mandatory Telework, non-essential personnel confined to residences.

I scrolled, my heart picking up speed. My portfolio couldn't afford to stop for locked gates; we funded the labs, the ARVs, and the clinics across the region. I cross-checked the President's essential services list against the Embassy cable. Health workers, laboratories, supply chains: I qualified. But the window for movement was closing fast.

I fired off a message to my team: Check every PEPFAR partner tonight. We need 21-day stock counts. If the trucks stop on Friday, we're in trouble.

Even as I hit send, a new alert blinked on my laptop: **GLOBAL LEVEL 4 – DO NOT TRAVEL.** I stared at the screen. This was no longer just a South African problem. It was a global dilemma. The world was officially shutting its doors.

Ramaphosa talked about deploying the South African National Defence Force to the streets to support the police. I remember thinking this was not going to work. This was South Africa, after all. They were experts at visible disasters: load-shedding that plunged cities into darkness, taxis torched over fare hikes, and potholes big enough to swallow tires. They dodged, adapted, and carried on. An invisible enemy and an "enforced lockdown"? It would be more of a suggestion than a rule. I waited for the defiance, the burning tires, and the hustlers who refuse to be told "no."

But Thursday midnight came, and South Africa didn't explode. It just stopped.

A strange silence greeted the next morning. Usually, the N1 highway hummed in the distance, leaf blowers whined, and the suburbs pulsed with motion. Now, there was only stillness. No cars. No sirens. Just hadedas screeching into the empty air. Even the hustlers stayed inside.

Twenty-one days stretched into forty-two. Each address from the President brought more weeks, more rules, and more waiting. We stopped pretending it was temporary. We learned how to live locked down and how to shrink our worlds. Before we knew it, the countdowns stopped mattering. This was not a pause. It was our new, warped normal, and we had to learn to survive within it.

While COVID-19 locked us behind our gates, another fever was burning across the Atlantic back home.

In May 2020, a video went viral showing a Black man named George Floyd being pinned to the pavement by a police officer in Minneapolis. As he whispered, then cried, "I can't breathe," the world was forced to confront a truth Black families have carried for generations. The footage of his final moments did not stay in America. It crossed oceans and landed in our diplomatic corridors like a shock wave. Inside, I was horrified and unraveled, imagining my beloved Anthony pinned beneath a system that would not see his humanity, gasping for air, for mercy, for recognition. That cry lodged itself in my heart then, and it has never fully left.

But this was not only a moment of mourning. It was a moment of reckoning.

As protests erupted across continents and governments issued statements of solidarity, I found myself reckoning with a hard reality: the language of diplomacy is often fluent in concern, yet slow to translate outrage into policy. I was serving in spaces where justice was discussed in measured tones, even as the world outside demanded urgency. George Floyd's final plea echoed in meeting rooms, policy briefs, and late-night reflections, forcing a question I could no longer avoid: what does accountability look like when the injustice is not distant, but domestic; not abstract, but deeply personal?

As a Black woman leading at a high level, I could not just "facilitate a meeting" about it. I had to acknowledge the blood in the water. I jumped in and helped create the Diversity, Equity, and Inclusion Working Group, with colleagues like Priya and Rebecca, and designed an Embassy-wide series called "Tell Your Story." It became a safe space where ambassadors and interns alike sat in the discomfort of our differences.

The work did not just double; it transformed. My laptop became a bridge between worlds. One tab was open to a spreadsheet of personal protective equipment (PPE) shipments to clinics in Qacha's Nek. The other was a "Tell Your Story" session where I listened to my colleagues weep over the state of the world. As an Officer, I had to be the anchor for both. I had to ensure the life-saving medication kept moving while also ensuring my team felt safe enough to breathe. We were operating at the highest levels of international diplomacy from our dining room tables. We were proving that the Mission did not live in a building in Pretoria.

The Mission lived in us.

While I was fighting to keep the Mission alive, my son was going through his own challenges. The schools had also completely shut down and moved to online learning. With Anthony's ADHD, virtual school was its own kind of struggle. Teachers tried, but nothing replaced the human spark his brain needed. No more balls bouncing on the basketball courts and no friends dropping by. His laugh grew quieter. Some days his camera stayed off, leaving just a black square where a vibrant kid used to be. On the hardest nights, I would find him in front of the house, shooting hoops alone in the dark. The ball thumped like a lonely heartbeat.

In that hush, we found our lifeline: Snoopy. Who would have known?

We built a routine around Snoopy to stay active and, frankly, sane. Every morning, we tackled the "killer hill," which was the impossibly steep driveway we used to curse. Now, it was our sanctuary. Anthony would sprint ahead, I would follow more slowly with my post-hip-replacement gait, and Snoopy would lead the charge, ears flopping like flags.

Middays, we would take a walk through the dog park and play with Snoopy there. That tiny Yorkie became our license to leave the house. Our property backed onto a dog park with a gate leading straight from our yard to the grass. It was our private portal to the outside world. We were luckier than most.

193

In the evenings, we cooked together, most times something easy I had picked up from the nearby Woolies shop or Anthony's favorite mac and cheese, just to keep our hands busy. I spent my mornings chairing inter-agency calls across various countries and my afternoons coaxing Anthony to keep going through frozen loading screens.

Walking that hill each day, I realized we were not just exercising. We were reclaiming ground. One steep step at a time, we proved the world had not gone completely silent. As long as we had that gate, that dog, and each other, we were still here. We were still a team. We were still moving.

But peace in a pandemic is a fragile thing. Just as we found our rhythm on that hill, my body decided to stop cooperating. One day, I woke up with a strange sensation in my hand. It felt like pins and needles. It soon progressed to burning electric shocks down my arm every time I turned my head. It was something I had never experienced before. I still remember how frantically I searched for unknown COVID-19 symptoms, hoping this was not one of them.

The pain got to a point where it forced me to go see my doctor. When I arrived, I was reluctant and expected him to tell me it was nothing major. I hoped a few pills and physical therapy would fix whatever was wrong. But in my world, extremes are the norm. The doctor ordered an MRI. When he pulled up the scan, the bulging discs in my neck looked like angry white tongues nearly pressing against my spinal cord.

"If we don't address this," he said quietly, "you risk paralysis. We need to go in and shave them down as soon as possible."

I was terrified. The timing couldn't have been worse. The world was hiding from a virus that seemed to lurk in every breath, and hospitals had become the last place anyone wanted to be. Yet here I was, a single mother in Pretoria, thousands of miles from family, facing surgery again. If I stayed locked behind our gates, I risked permanent paralysis. If I went in, I risked catching the very thing we were all running from. Knife or wheelchair, those were the options. I chose the knife.

The morning of the surgery, the antiseptic smell hit me like a memory I didn't want. Same scent as 2017, only now layered with new fear in 2021. I drifted off, counting ceiling tiles, and woke up several hours later, throat raw, feeling like I'd swallowed a rock.

For six weeks, I wore a hard plastic collar that made me look like an alien. Swallowing was a chore. I couldn't lift my arms past my shoulders. The "Officer-in-Charge" became a woman in bed, waiting for other people to carry her, literally and otherwise.

This time Judith was my lifeline. She blended soups thin enough to sip through a straw and never once sighed when I asked for the same thing twice. Anthony stepped up in ways that warmed my heart. He learned to gather my hair into a ponytail because I couldn't reach it, his fingers careful and surprisingly gentle for a teenage boy. Some afternoons, I'd lie there listening to jacaranda petals tap the roof during summer storms, wondering how my kid had become the steady one.

Friends from USAID and the neighborhood showed up too, food dropped at the gate, group chat messages that made me laugh until my neck protested. Nya Kwai and Ann, whom I had met in Tanzania and were also now working in South Africa, brought me some beautiful flowers and soup. For the first time in years, I let myself lean on the village I'd built across continents. In that stillness, collar clicking with every small movement, I realized the support had always been there. I'd just never let myself need it before.

Even with the neck brace locked around my throat, I refused to let the work stall.

When the previous Lesotho Country Director took authorized departure and never returned, it left a hole no one else seemed ready to immediately fill. Still healing, throat raw from the collar, I stepped in anyway, acting in that position until I could find a replacement. I recruited across time zones, rewrote job descriptions between pain-med doses, and chaired interview panels with CDC colleagues while my eyes blurred from the screen. I was rebuilding a team at the same time my own spine was being rebuilt.

Hospitals in South Africa and Lesotho were drowning. I knew that if we paused even for a moment, COVID would erase every hard-won gain against HIV. I went into full Director mode, lobbying Washington, pressing the Department of Defense, consulting the WHO, and the World Bank. I pushed ahead with my funding proposal until an additional $1 million came through for PPE and oxygen concentrators.

Meanwhile, staff morale across the mission had sunk to rock bottom. It was one of the lowest scores USAID had ever recorded through its annual survey. Spreadsheets and budgets weren't enough anymore. I mentored young officers, pushed harder on Diversity Days, and kept reminding everyone that we would never outspend this epidemic, so we had to out-think it.

Somehow, through lockdowns, surgeries, and sheer stubbornness, my team and I pushed Lesotho to the brink of the impossible. We hit the UNAIDS 90-90-90 targets and achieved HIV epidemic control, a milestone celebrated around the world. The three nineties meant diagnosing nearly everyone living with HIV, ensuring almost all of those diagnosed received treatment, and suppressing the virus so completely that transmission all but stopped.

At the same time, my surgeons begged me to slow down. I couldn't. People were learning how to breathe again, and I wasn't about to step away from that. The world needed me even when I was at my most fragile. Actually, the world needed all of us. We realized in those dark months just how much we needed each other. We proved we could live and conquer as a global family, no matter how hard the lockdowns got. We were finding our way through a storm that had no map, and we were doing it together.

Then, the seasons shifted. The virus was brought under control, and the world slowly reopened its doors again. Nothing, it turns out, stays permanent. Borders reopened. Schools called the kids back. Anthony had missed his prom, but he was not going to miss his walk across that graduation stage. My mom and Nancy flew in from the States. Joe came from Tanzania. One of Anthony's uncles drove all the way from Limpopo just to be there and cheer him on.

It was a clear June day, the sky was a perfect blue and the sun a radiant yellow. The parking lot was buzzing with activity as we pulled in and found a spot. The school auditorium was set up at two-thirds capacity: chairs taped into careful social distancing islands, two meters apart. Mom clutched her purse and pulled out a red and white peppermint. Nancy balanced her phone in one hand and her lip gloss in the other, trying to get a perfect shot.

When Anthony's name crackled over the PA system, the small crowd erupted. There were cheers and ululations, and even one vuvuzela someone had kept since the 2010 World Cup. I stood up and simply lifted both arms in the air, saying, "There's my baby, thank you, God."

He crossed the stage in his gown and kente cloth sash, diploma in one hand, the other tucked behind his back. He looked proud. Watching him, I realized South Africa hadn't just taught me lessons. It had shaped him, too. He'd lived through the revised school rules of lockdown and the lonely nights on the basketball court, but he had pushed through. We both had. We'd been brought to our knees and learned, together, how to stand back up.

We weren't just surviving our "new normal" that had started when he was four years old. We were thriving in it. Even with one man missing, we were still a complete team. We were no longer just an officer and her son. We were two survivors who had found their breath in a world that had tried to take it away.

Despite the isolation of lockdowns and the heaviness of that season, my social life in South Africa quietly reassembled itself in ways that surprised me. I reunited with old Peace Corps friends and reconnected with members of my host family from Limpopo, including Thabo, who was my little brother. The boy I remembered trailing behind us was now a grown man, a confident engineer working for an international company based in Johannesburg, traveling across the region to service diamond mines. There was also

Phemelo, my little sister, who is now a Communications professional in the non-profit sector. Watching them move through the world with purpose and ease felt like a full-circle moment, a reminder that the seeds planted years ago had taken root in ways I could not have imagined.

When friends visited, like Palesa, Moroka, Thulani, Waahida, Zolisa, and countless others, our home became a gathering place. I was even reunited with friends from my Tanzania days, like Marc, Teresa, and Mandisa, who had also made South Africa their home. We hosted braais that stretched into long afternoons and unhurried evenings, out back surrounding the fire pit, with laughter carrying through the house and music floating in from the yard. Those moments mattered. They grounded me. In a time when so much felt uncertain, opening our doors and breaking bread together restored a sense of normalcy and belonging. Community, even in small doses, became a form of medicine.

I also carried the sadness of suddenly losing a friend, Jabulani Tsambo, the artist known to many as HHP, whom I had met years earlier in Washington, D.C. His death in 2018 left behind his son, Leano, and something about that loss still lingers with me. Leano resembles Anthony, a gentle reminder of how fragile our existence can be, and how much presence and care matter.

Out of my own need for connection, I created a WhatsApp group called Sisters of South Africa. What began as a modest support system to help me navigate my transition into life there quickly took on a life of its own. Women invited other women, questions became advice, and advice became reassurance. Over time, the group grew into a lifeline for so many, including La Chenna, Meisha, Kim and Xima, as they navigated relocation, reinvention, heartbreak, career shifts, and joy. To this day, it has grown to over three hundred members. I'm thankful for friends like Kenna and Eshanda who help me manage it. Watching it flourish reminded me how powerful it is when women create space for one another, especially far from home.

Anthony, too, found his rhythm. He joined the Jr. NBA league, and weekends were soon filled with basketball games, early mornings, and the familiar rituals of being a sports mom. I loved watching him on the court, alongside other moms like Edith and Memuna, confident and focused, carving out his place. Beyond sports, he was also discovering South Africa in his own way. I felt a quiet joy watching him gravitate toward Afrohouse and Amapiano music, seeing him lean into a cultural inheritance that felt both new and deeply familiar.

Lockdown also gave Anthony an unexpected gift: time to turn inward. With the world slowed and the noise turned down, he began writing his own music, rapping over beats he found online, experimenting and finding his voice. One of my favorite songs is titled "Zanzibar" and it was heartening to know that he also had love for my favorite island. He recorded an EP and started sharing his songs on social media under the name FG Tony, with FG standing for Fierce Gang, a reflection of both his mindset and the leisurewear brand he designed and sold during that same season.

In those moments, I could see him stitching together parts of himself, finding pride and curiosity in his South African roots, and, more than anything, that made that chapter of our lives feel rich and whole.

We also had fun together, going to plays and concerts across Gauteng, immersing ourselves in the country's vibrant music and theater scene. One memorable moment was watching a brilliant play directed by my friend Palesa, featuring another friend, Zizi, as the lead actor. I had the pleasure of introducing Anthony to my old stomping grounds in Yeoville, where we shared a delicious Pan-African meal at the famed supper club hosted by the ever-charismatic Sanza.

We played tour guide to visitors from home like Stephanie and Alison, taking them to iconic sites such as Soweto, the Apartheid Museum, Maboneng, Cape Town vineyards, and safari parks. In a country marked by beauty and struggle, Anthony found the other half of his roots, and I found my footing the second time around.

A month later, we packed the house for the last time. The logistics were a bit more complicated than usual. Anthony was heading to college in Maryland, I was bound for South Sudan, and most of our household effects would be sent to storage in Belgium. For the first time since he was born, we were not going together.

But there was one more family member to consider, Snoopy.

"Mom, Snoopy is coming with me," Anthony said. There was no question mark and no room for debate.

I looked at my son, taller now with a deep baritone voice that came out of nowhere, and then at the little Yorkie who had marched every inch of that killer hill with us.

"Anthony, the flights, the permits, the quarantine rules. It is a lot. Maybe we can find him a good home here? Someone with a big garden?"

"No. He is my dog. He got us through lockdown. I am not leaving him behind."

He did not budge, and I realized he was right. Snoopy was not just a pet we had picked up along the way. He was our witness. He was the one who kept us moving when the world stopped spinning.

We wrestled the red tape, the crates, and the vet clearances. We were no longer leaving as a duo. We were a trio. Thankfully, his aunt Nancy agreed to take Snoopy in while we both embarked on our new journeys.

We checked into the Johannesburg departures hall together, but it felt different this time. I watched Anthony handle his two huge suitcases and his basketball with a steady, quiet confidence. He was the one double-checking Snoopy's crate and making sure the water bowl was secure.

Even though we were boarding the same flight to the States for a visit before I flew to my new posting in South Sudan, the shift had already happened. I watched him move through the security line ahead of me. He was tall, South African-American, with Limpopo dust in his veins, America in his bones, and Haiti in his laugh. He did not look back to see if I was following. He did not need to. He was heading toward his future with his sanity saver at his side, and for the first time, he was leading the way.

I stood in the queue, one hand on the hip South Africa had rebuilt. This posting had made me pay the bill for every mile I had traveled. I had done it while limping. I had done it while calling Maryland every night to say goodnight to a mother who sometimes knew my name and sometimes did not. I had even done it while swallowing the fear that the next surgery or midnight call might finally ground me.

It never did. The neck brace was gone, but its memory still straightened my spine.

I was no longer the young, naive volunteer who had arrived in Limpopo, nor was I the woman who had limped off the plane in Joburg thinking she had to be unbreakable. I was the sum of every crash, every surgery, and every grandmother's smile in Mohale's Hoek. I was proof that broken bones could still carry a mission across the finish line. In many ways, South Africa mirrored life itself: complicated and beautiful, still struggling, yet animated by a spirit that believes tomorrow can be better than today.

Hi again, bye again, southern Africa. Thank you for every hard, beautiful, impossible lesson.

I am still standing, and I am still moving forward.

Our little pooch Snoopy, who provided much-needed comfort during those long days.

Chapter Fifteen

SMALL MIRACLES INSIDE A METAL BOX

The Ethiopian Airlines flight was packed to the brim, full of families with screaming babies and oversized carry-on baggage. Strapped tightly into my seat, I closed my eyes and repeated the numbers that had become my quiet version of a prayer over the past several months after I received my new assignment. Stagnant maternal mortality ratio, one of the highest in the world; 1.5 million people reached with water and sanitation; a portfolio just shy of forty million dollars. I was going to be the Health Office Director for the first time. My mind was supposed to run like a balance sheet, always reconciling to targets and indicators while taking care of my team and monitoring the quality of the programs supporting community members.

This new assignment was going to be like nothing I had ever experienced before. A heavy sense of gravity set in, as it typically does when I move to a new country. I had felt that gravity in South Africa, watching a wall rise one cinder block at a time. I had wrestled supply chains across Tanzania's red dirt roads and the paperwork that multiplied faster than malaria in the wet season. I had watched a typhoon erase five years of work in the Philippines. I had even managed a team in Lesotho who paddled dugout canoes through uncharted waters to deliver antiretrovirals. By then, I believed I understood what hard places looked like.

But none of them prepared me for Juba. Not even close.

As I sat on that flight, the briefings still echoed in my mind, but so did the kid from Queens who lived in the back of my head. She had her own way of cutting through the noise. *You think you have seen tough. This is different.* And she was right.

Before I had even booked a ticket to a place like South Sudan, the warnings lined up.

"It's unstable."

"It's dangerous."

"You will live in a shipping container."

"Do not drive. Ever."

Our training tells us to nod and stick to the facts without showing any emotion. But travel gives you far too much time to think. I found myself chewing on stereotypes, specifically those that never mention the people who laugh, fall in love, and raise children while life happens all around them. I wondered if I would be safe. I told myself the training prepared me, but then I had to admit, very quietly, that no handbook teaches you how it feels when bullets whiz by at a moment's notice.

Still, I had chosen this. Partly to serve, yes, but also to see the world with my own eyes. No filters. No headlines. Just the truth.

When the pilot announced our descent, I opened my eyes. The view through the small window shifted slowly into focus. Rust red earth stretched beautifully out in all directions, flat and wide, the color of iron filings. Greenery lined a long, winding waterway, which the pilot announced was the Nile River. The scenery then quickly switched to what seemed like millions of tin roofs packed together side by side. It felt like the field's first lesson whispering to me. South

Sudan does not follow rules.

The plane dropped hard, and then the engines settled into a long, tired silence. A rattling bus carried us across the tarmac, and when I stepped onto the ground, the heat slapped the back of my throat like a cast-iron pan. It carried wood smoke, and underneath that, the faint smell of the earth itself.

I stood there a moment longer than usual. For the first time in twenty years, I was on foreign soil without my mother or my son by my side. Anthony was safely tucked into his college dorm for his freshman year. My mother was in her seniors-only apartment. Both in Maryland, not too far away from Nancy. The rules of this high-threat post did not allow family members, which created a clean break I had not fully expected. And for the first time in years, I could leave without worrying about who I was leaving behind. Somewhat guilt-free.

The arrival sequence broke every familiar pattern I had known over the years. In all my other posts, my welcome always followed the same warm script. A cheerful embassy driver. A clean, high clearance SUV. A US Embassy sign with my name written in hopeful block letters. A short exchange of pleasantries that settled the nerves after long flights and intimidating immigration lines.

Here, none of that applied.

When I got off the transit bus, an older South Sudanese man approached me as soon as my feet hit the tarmac again.

"Ms. Jennifer?" he asked.

I said yes, and he grabbed my carry-on bag faster than I could say hello. He walked so fast I had to do a small jog to keep up.

As we approached the building, I couldn't believe this was the Juba International Airport. It didn't look like any other airport I had been to before; it looked like a patchwork of tents and aluminum. He took my passport, whisked me through customs and immigration without stopping, bypassing what felt like hundreds of giants jammed against each other. I was in awe at how tall and lean everyone was. Real model material. All I could think about at that moment was how there was no way I was going to blend in here.

We were outside again in under 5 minutes flat, under the most unforgiving sun I had met to date.

An armored Land Cruiser rolled up out of nowhere, its tires spitting red dust in sharp little bursts. The driver jumped out, threw my carry-on into the trunk, and opened the back door for me to get in. I was so confused because I hadn't even picked up my two suitcases yet. The expediter caught the panic on my face and grinned as wide as the Nile. He had a gap in his teeth bigger than mine. When I saw that I knew I was home again and my anxiety started to fade.

He said, "Don't worry, my sister. Your bags will find you at the compound." Then he gave the driver a single nod. I climbed in with my backpack, and the heavy door shut behind me with the finality of a bank vault closing for the night.

What followed felt like a slow introduction to the rules of this new world. We drove through the compound gates wrapped in barbed wire after a thorough security check, past guards who looked ready to shoot first and hold their questions for the inquisition.

When the vehicle finally stopped, it was on a patch of clean gravel. I stepped out and saw my new home. Two shipping containers stacked and welded together, one bedroom with an ensuite bathroom, a living/dining room combo, and a kitchenette small enough to fit one person. I ran my hand along the metal wall. Beige. Warm from the sun already.

Only a few months ago, I was turning the key to a two-story house in Pretoria while jacaranda petals drifted onto my manicured lawn. And here I was, living in a metal box where I could hear my neighbor cough through the floor. To stay calm, I thought back to the rondavels where I slept during long field trips in South Africa. I reminded myself that I once survived on a thin mattress in one room in Limpopo. If I got through those Peace Corps days, I could certainly get through this.

My new reality had me living on the only US compound in town, which worked like a small, self-contained universe. There was a restaurant, a swimming pool, and a gym. On paper, it sounded almost like a resort. In real life, it was more like a box with Wi Fi.

Our world shrank to three permitted paths. Walk down one block to the embassy. Walk to the grocery store across the embassy's back entrance. Walk back. Curfew was seven in the evening, sharp, every single night. I never saw Juba after dark, not once.

It was a strange adjustment. In Tanzania, I had followed music down dirt roads until sunrise, dancing with strangers who felt like old friends by morning. Now I managed a forty-million-dollar portfolio and still could not cross a street without a literal security clearance. I had to move everywhere with my Emergency and Evacuation embassy-issued radio and check in upon departure and arrival every single time. My UN and private sector friends, like Timmie, Frida, Raphael, and Jessie Ann, would text the next day, wishing I had joined them. Apparently, the city after dark was very much alive. I would smile, delete the message, and accept the quiet. The curfew was less about bullets and more about police checkpoints that bloomed after dark, apparently, looking for foreigners with cash. I had been bold at nineteen. I was long past the age when invincibility felt like a birthright. I had a son starting college and a mother who needed me more than anything. I intended to go home to them.

So, I learned how to live a large life inside a small box.

Most mornings began before the sun. Routine was the one thing I controlled. The air was still cool enough to breathe without effort. Generators hummed across the compound, steady and almost soothing. I stepped outside in boots or sneakers and yesterday's dust. Gravel crunched under my feet, the only sound for a few seconds.

The dining hall offered eggs and coffee strong enough to wake even the bravest souls. Taisha, another USAID officer, slid into the chair beside me.

"First morning?" she asked.

"Yes, and it's been very quiet," I said.

"It'll get quieter. Then you'll get used to it. We all do."

And she was right. You have to.

My substitute life began the next morning. I slipped into it the way you slip into a routine you did not ask for but accept anyway.

At dawn, I joined the walkers and runners who circled inside the fence, chasing off the static that collected behind my knees. The real refuge was the gym: clanging weights, thumping treadmills, one hour when the razor wire faded. There, I met Mark, a Marine built with the general proportions of a small bridge.

"Five forty-five or you owe me burpees," he said, half grin, half drill sergeant.

I never missed again. If I could survive hours-long donor meetings, I could survive his circuits. The workouts became my pocket of normal inside the container life.

When the hour ended, I wiped the dust from my skin and walked to the office, time to trade sweat for spreadsheets, and push the maternal-mortality line instead of my heart rate.

The USAID office was small, so it was housed inside the US Embassy and carried the same security posture as the compound. I led the USAID health team, a tight group of about ten. Half were brilliant South Sudanese physicians, like Basilica, who had been with the mission since day one. We managed the major programs: HIV and AIDS, maternal and child health, family planning, global health security, and water and sanitation. Most of our work happened outside Juba, scattered across states and counties, but, for physical and safety reasons, we could not simply drive to monitor our programs as we could in other countries.

Every trip was a month-long paperwork saga: security clearances, flight requests, a cargo hold of sorghum sacks we wedged between.

Paved roads had long since given way to ruts and no longer existed outside Juba, so we flew UN World Food Program helicopters or prop planes meant for food drops. I sat on the tiniest seats I've ever seen, helmet between my knees, counting rivets like rosary beads, today, tomorrow, any day the sky might object. Ambush wasn't just a probability; we were told it was always the biggest threat.

We landed to a greeting circle of blue helmets, rifles slung, ready to lead our convoy. Aisha waited outside the prop wash, white coat snapping in the rotor wind. She caught my wrist and pulled me close.

"Director, if USAID leaves, we close tomorrow, and people will die."

I placed my arm around her shoulders, "I know," I said. "I know what happens if we leave. That's why I'm not letting it happen on my watch."

The promise tasted of dust and adrenaline; I swallowed both.

I knew, too, that some of the same hands waving at the clinic had quietly restocked their own shelves, a few vials of antibiotics traded for school-fee receipts, and I swallowed that knowledge with the same gulp. We counted bed nets, photographed the incubator that had become a warming drawer, and promised spare parts. The staff waved us off like departing cousins, their smiles narrow but unbroken. Within a few hours, we were back on the plane. We had to get back before dark because security wouldn't let us stay overnight, and there were no runway lights in Juba. I wedged my bulletproof vest under my seat and let the engine vibration drill the sentence into my ribs: stay, stay, stay, you can do this.

Below, the brown earth kept its secrets. Every circle of thatch roof was a wager against gravity; my spreadsheet cells felt suddenly flimsy, the looks of every mom and baby I had just seen on the long queues forever etched into my heart. I reminded myself of the promise I made back in Tanzania: never look away.

The plane landed, the sun caught the propeller, and I felt the balance shift, the weight of need heavier than fear, heavier than the vest now crumpled at my feet like shed skin.

Some trips leave scars; others leave hope. No matter which one it was, I carried them home.

Another time, we flew to a women's shea butter cooperative. I sat on a plastic stool while they showed me how they cracked the nuts, boiled the mash, and skimmed the oil.

Watching the women operate the shea press was like witnessing a quiet revolution. These were the same women who, previously, had walked past the fallen nuts under the trees, their days so consumed by survival that even abundance could go unnoticed at their feet. Now they stood side by side, not just as workers but as owners of their future. Their conversation was about more than how much butter they could produce. It was about what it meant to control their own labor and share in the reward, providing brighter futures for their children.

We bought jugs of that thick, golden butter along with other products. For a moment, the numbers on my spreadsheets stopped feeling abstract. This was more than funding. It was a lifeline, a bridge from survival to dignity. It reminded me that the real work was not just about health statistics or budgets but about helping people reclaim the power they had quietly carried all along.

Most days were not that simple or hopeful, though.

I remember one meeting in particular, held in an Internally Displaced Persons camp managed by the UN just outside Juba. It was not a refugee camp in the usual sense, but felt like one. These were South Sudanese families who had fled violence in the northern and other regional states, seeking whatever safety they could find near the capital. The camp had grown into a more than just temporary city of tents and tin structures. Our humanitarian office worked there often, so visits had become part of our regular rhythm.

From a distance, the camp looked steady. But there was no access to water or firewood inside the walls. To cook or even just survive, people had to leave the relative safety of the camp and go outside, where armed groups still moved around the community. Every trip was a risk.

We sat under a canvas shade to talk about water and sanitation with a group of ten camp elders, all male except one. The conversation quickly turned to who would be responsible for collecting water outside the protected area. One of the men, clearly the community leader, spoke firmly. He said the men couldn't be the ones to make those trips because if they left the perimeter, the fighting forces might kill them.

I stared at him, unable to accept what he was saying. My chest tightened as I tried to process the blunt arithmetic of his position. You value your life above the safety of your women, I thought. I looked around at the other men, all nodding in agreement. They were not talking about chores. They were talking about who was expendable in their political and physical reality. I wanted to speak, to rage at the reduction of women to acceptable losses, but years of Foreign Service training reminded me that I was there to observe and propose, not impose. I nodded, kept my face neutral, and bit my tongue, literally.

Well, one of my colleagues did not. The whole atmosphere shifted dramatically.

"So it is fine if the women get raped or killed?!" she fumed.

Everything tightened in the space of a heartbeat. The men's faces hardened. Our security officers shifted their stances, their hands moving toward their belts. My pulse raced. I felt the situation tilting, sharp as a blade, and thought: We are ten kilometers from the compound, surrounded, and everyone here might be carrying a gun or two under his shirt.

I remained silent. It was instinct as much as training. My colleague believed she was standing up for women. I believed we were one sentence from a disaster, and no amount of moral clarity would help us if we pushed too far in the wrong moment.

Eventually, the heat settled. Voices softened. Our security detail retreated a bit. We finished the discussion, closed our notebooks, and walked back to the vehicles surrounded by human shields, with our hearts still thudding.

As we drove through the checkpoints on the way back, I understood something I had never put into words before. This work was not only about budgets, logistics, or medical commodities. It was also about sitting in circles like that one, holding back the scream in my throat, and choosing the response that kept the clinic open the next day. Some days, courage is loud. Other days it is quiet. And on the hardest days, it simply looks like making it home alive so you can keep fighting tomorrow.

The work that stayed with me was never the mortality curves. It was my DREAMS girls. I had to keep my eyes on the prize.

Just like in Tanzania, this program sat under the HIV portfolio and focused on vulnerable teenage girls, many of whom were already single mothers, offering them life skills and vocational training. The program in Juba taught skills like tailoring, hair braiding, and culinary arts, practical training that could guarantee them a path to self-reliance by generating some income. I attended every graduation I could. The girls would walk across the dust-filled courtyard in caps and gowns and new uniforms, shoulders squared, eyes bright with the hope that could lift a whole row of plastic chairs.

After the ceremonies, many struggled to find steady work. Most tried to set up a small sewing station under a tree or open a tiny salon. Then the sewing machine would break, the customers would dry up, and by the six-month mark, they were back at the start. It was heartbreaking to watch the enthusiasm for their micro businesses fade.

Then a lifeline appeared. In May 2022, the Radisson Hotel Group opened its first location in Juba. For us at the embassy, it felt like a minor vacation spot, twenty minutes from the compound. One afternoon, I was sitting there with a burger that almost tasted like home, and I ended up chatting with Vijay, the HR manager.

I asked, "Are you hiring?"

He laughed. "We are just opening up. We are hiring everybody."

That was all I needed. I returned to the office and pitched a collaboration idea to my colleague Takele on the Economic Growth team. What if we built a public-private partnership that placed our DREAMS girls inside the Radisson for actual jobs? He perked up. We consulted Washington colleagues and passed the idea by our senior leaders. Haven and Michele loved it. I drafted a short concept note for a six-week paid internship in real departments with real training, with the possibility of a full-time job upon successful completion. We pitched it, and Vijay called back two days later and asked to meet.

"We do this in Nigeria and India all the time. Send us resumes."

Our partner NGO helped prepare the girls. They practiced interviews and printed resumes. We sent twenty. The Radisson selected ten.

On the first morning, I arrived early. I watched the girls enter the lobby, trying to stand tall while looking like they wished the tiles would open up and swallow them. They were nervous. For most of them, this would be the only chance they'd get to walk into this kind of establishment.

Vijay welcomed them, and the girls were assigned to their departments. Agnes, a single mother with a contagious laugh, went into engineering. I checked in throughout the day and watched nerves shift into focus. At one point, I saw a maintenance man teaching Agnes how to handle the generators. She asked if she could try. John handed her a wrench, and from across the room I watched her tighten the bolts with a steady hand. She looked up, her face lit with pride, and said, "I did it."

Not everything went smoothly. One girl became pregnant and had to leave.

Another's husband stormed in and demanded she come home. While he waited for her to collect her things, I watched her every movement tighten. Her shoulders folded inward, her eyes stayed fixed on the floor, and her silence said everything. It was not a failure. It was a public loss.

I stood there in my blazer, feeling completely useless. I had moved budgets, approvals, concept papers, and emails across three time zones, yet I could not stop one man from walking in and taking away her future. It reminded me of the child marriages I had witnessed in Tanzania, where girls were traded for dowries and their futures locked away before they even began. The Radisson lobby looked modern, but the dynamic was painfully familiar. I already knew the statistic: one in three women nationwide, but statistics don't sit in your gut with a pulse and a face.

Then there was the girl caught taking shampoo and a bit of cash from a guest room. I felt a knot in my stomach when I heard.

Vijay was more relaxed. "We expected a few losses in the first round," he said with a shrug. "Seven out of ten is a win. Don't worry."

Despite everything, seven completed the internship, and four were hired permanently. Now and then, I still get a WhatsApp message from one of the girls, Flora, smiling in her crisp Radisson uniform, standing next to a cake she baked or a VIP she checked in. The hotel continued the program long after I left.

There were other girls in the program, too. I went to see a hair salon that a few of them had started. The place was just a tiny shack. It was so small that only two hairdressers and two clients could fit inside at once. The rest of the girls had to wait outside and rotate in when it was their turn to work. Sitting there with them, I was moved by their joy, and I couldn't hold back my tears. Even in that cramped little space, they were so grateful and happy to be building something of their own. I felt proud to have helped them start that dream, no matter how small it was.

As I watched them, I looked at every hand, every face, and every smile. I realized that nothing really separated us except geography. It was a lottery ticket picked for me without my choosing. I couldn't stop thinking about how easily that could have been my life. If I had been born in a different coordinate, I could have been the one in that shack.

In that moment, I felt a real oneness with them. I realized my mission was not about saving anyone. It was about standing together in that oneness and saying, *I see you. I hear you. I am here for you.* We were in this together. In Africa, they call it Ubuntu: I am because you are. In Haiti, we say *Men anpil, chay pa lou*—many hands make the load light. There was no distance between us. I was them, and they were me.

Looking back on fifteen years at USAID, the DREAMS projects felt like the best work I ever pulled off. In a country where almost nothing worked, those girls showed me that the improbable is actually possible. Occasionally, a miracle emerges that manages to stay glued together, even in the humidity.

Beyond the larger programs, we also supported smaller, local efforts like a community orphanage on the outskirts of town. It was a place for children who had lost their parents to conflict and disease.

During one of our monitoring visits, the local partners gathered the kids under a mango tree with plastic chairs arranged in tidy rows. A few brief speeches followed. I smiled, nodded, and clapped.

Then they brought up a girl who looked about six or seven years old. She was tiny. Her dress slipped off one shoulder and dragged in the dust. Someone lowered the microphone. She held it with both hands.

She looked right at us, locking eyes with me, Kevin, and our other mission colleagues.

"My mother and father died in the fighting," she said. "My brothers, too. I stayed with my grandmother, but she is sick, and there was no food. Sometimes I only ate leaves."

I thought of my own son at that age, worried about nothing more than dirty sneakers.

She continued. "Now I sleep on a mattress, not on the ground. I eat every day. And I go to school."

She lifted her chin slightly. "Thank you, Madam Director. Thank you, USAID! Shukran."

My eyes filled so fast I had to look down at my hands. When I looked up again, she was walking toward me, her dress grazing the ground.

I thought of Agnes fixing generators. I thought of every spreadsheet I had ever written to fight for one more dollar for this country. None of it felt big enough anymore. My throat tightened. I crouched.

"What's your name?"

"Rebecca."

"Rebecca, you keep studying hard, okay? I'm proud of you."

She gave me the smallest polite smile and the biggest hug, and went back to her seat. I stood up, turned away fast, and wiped my face with the heel of my hand before anyone could notice the American Director crying in the red dust. Some moments live in you forever. Rebecca is one of mine.

My experience in the Philippines had taught me that two years was the minimum to see real traction. Plenty of colleagues counted the days until their mandatory one-year tour in Juba was over, but I signed up for another year without flinching. I am grateful I did. Watching our programs literally save lives and watching my team hold the line every day made the decision feel almost effortless.

South Sudan, I've since learned, is a place that stays with you long after you leave it. It is raw and unfinished, heavy with history and hope in equal measure. Life there feels close to the surface, intense, unfiltered, deeply human. The land is wide and sun-scorched, the sky impossibly big, and the Nile moves through it all like a quiet witness, carrying stories older than the country itself. There is struggle everywhere you look, yes, but also resilience that humbles you: laughter that breaks through hardship, generosity offered without excess, and people who keep showing up for one another despite everything they have endured. In South Sudan, nothing is abstract. Conflict, peace, joy, fear, friendship all live side by side. It is a place that teaches you presence, strips away pretense, and reminds you how powerful it is simply to bear witness and care.

Leaving South Sudan affected me in a way I hadn't fully prepared for. In just two years, far too short for a place that asks so much of you, I had built a family that spanned borders: South Sudanese friends who welcomed me with warmth and resilience, and fellow foreigners who became kin through shared intensity, humor, and survival. There was no way I was slipping out quietly. I needed one last gathering that felt like us, so I hosted my signature all-white farewell party, a ritual I'd carried with me from Tanzania to South Africa and now here. Poolside at the Radisson, under a sky heavy with heat and humidity, DJ E kept the rhythm alive as people from every walk of life showed up. No hierarchy, no IDs, no titles, no pretenses. We drank champagne the hotel had mistakenly given us instead of sparkling wine (a happy accident we laughed about all night), ate Chef Dinesh's delicious chocolate cake, and danced without holding back.

Sweat soaked through our white clothes, hair frizzed, makeup melted, but none of it mattered. It was joy, pure and unfiltered, a love fest. When the clock crept toward curfew, I danced right up until the last possible moment, then jumped back into the armored Land Cruiser to make it to the compound by 7 p.m., leaving behind those free to stay, to keep dancing, to stretch the night a little longer. As we pulled away, music fading into the thick air, I knew I wasn't just leaving a post, I was departing a place and the people in it who had lodged themselves permanently in my heart.

On my last morning, after serving two years, I walked the compound in the early light. The gravel still crunched under my sneakers, the generators still hummed, and the red dust still settled on my skin before the sun made up its mind. I thought about the fights I had chosen on purpose, like pushing the system to promote our South Sudanese Senior Health Advisor to Deputy Director. Her steady leadership would still be here long after the next American badge came through the gate. I thought about my team, the doctors, drivers, community volunteers, and logisticians who had not seen their villages in years because the road home was a lottery of roadblocks, gaping potholes, and gunfire. I thought about the small mental-health program we quietly started at the office, something everyone on the ground desperately needed.

Mostly, I thought about the people who kept showing up anyway.

Of course, the big systems stayed broken. Children still died for lack of a ten-cent vaccine. Roads washed out the week after we fixed them. Yet the small things continued anyway. A joke. A paycheck. A perfect jump shot.

I remembered the women under the shea trees laughing. I saw the basketball court where, with the Luol Deng Foundation, we had sponsored a life skills program for five hundred kids in new jerseys, screaming like the NBA had relocated. Saree, a newly found sister-friend from California, had joined me in handing out certificates to the enthusiastic young people who had gone through the program. Part of what made the experience a memory to cherish was the presence of Luol Deng himself. A son of the soil and former NBA star, he had walked in that day, tall and gentle, shaking hands as if every child mattered equally because they did.

When it was time to leave South Sudan, I left the compound the same way I arrived, in an armored convoy, passing through the final checkpoints. My heart felt heavier, but it also felt truer. South Sudan had stripped away the illusion that I or any foreigner could fix a place like this. Like everywhere else I worked, change had to come from within. What I could do was refuse to abandon it in spirit.

There is a saying that "once you drink from the River Nile, you'll always come back," so we shall see.

My souvenir shirt and the framed group photo of my DREAMS girls and me from my South Sudan farewell party.

Saying a final goodbye to friends at my South Sudan farewell party.

Connecting with Luol Deng at the Jr. NBA launch at the Radisson Hotel in Juba.

Chapter Sixteen

BANGKOK BEFORE THE BREAK

Twenty-six years is a long time to spend looking up. Since my Peace Corps days, I've been reaching for the next assignment, the next mission, the next horizon.

I stood at the floor-to-ceiling windows of my corner office on the twenty-sixth floor in Bangkok, my arms folded in the exact pose I had always imagined for a director. For more than a quarter of a century, I had moved through the world of international aid. I had seen more countries than I could count on my fingers and toes combined. But as I looked out at the shimmering expanse of the city, for the first time in my life, I didn't just feel like I was working; I felt like I was thriving.

If only my mother could see me now. I thought I had made it. I could hear The Jeffersons theme song in the back of my head, "We're moving up on to the East side."

Only months ago, my world had been a dust bowl of unpaved roads and red dust, defined by the constant, grinding struggle for existence. Now, I was at the helm of a regional operation coveted by many, housed in a magnificent, eco-friendly, award-winning skyscraper, all glass, vertical gardens, and high-tech everything.

My office was double the size of anything I'd ever occupied. In one corner sat a massive executive desk; in another, a formal table with four chairs arranged perfectly to receive visitors. The room was flooded with magnificent sunlight, that brilliant, high-altitude light that only the top of a skyscraper can capture.

Beyond the glass, the city of Bangkok sprawled out like a dream, a megalopolis of soaring steel and ancient buildings. I couldn't see the Chao Phraya River from my office, but I knew it was snaking through the center like a silk ribbon. Tucked between the modern towers were the rooftops of shining golden temples, sparkling in the sun.

I thought about the girl I used to be, growing up in Queens and watching the Manhattan skyline from across the water. Back then, those towers felt like a different world, an impossible one. Now, after over two decades of climbing, I wasn't just looking at the skyline; I was part of it.

But no matter how perfect the pinnacle looks in pictures, reaching it is never as effortless as it seems. I had given my best to the world, serving communities with everything I had, but I hadn't exactly breezed through it. My body was still presenting the bill for the climb. I could feel the sharp, pricking arthritis protest in my knees from time to time if I pushed them too much. Sporadically, my hand had that familiar, ghostly tingling, mostly overnight, and I found myself offering up a silent, continuous prayer: Please, don't let those shaved-down disks find their way back toward my spine again.

But the heaviest weight wasn't in my knees or neck; it was in my heart.

More than anything, I wanted the woman who started this journey with me to see where we had finally landed. But my mother was thousands of miles away in a care facility, slipping deeper into dementia every day. When we spoke, she didn't even recognize me. In her small, quiet voice, she'd call me by her dead sister's name and plead with me to take her home to her own mother, who also passed away a long time ago. It felt surreal.

Standing in that bright, modern office, I had to learn to hold both the sharp grief for the mother I was losing and the quiet pride in the life I had built. They lived side by side in my chest, neither one canceling the other out.

I turned away from the window and looked at the four chairs waiting for my first guests. I felt out of place if I were to be completely honest, but as I sat down at that massive desk, I knew I was exactly where I was meant to be.

People often ask how I landed such a coveted post. In the world of USAID, Bangkok is the best of the best, a place everyone vies for but few actually reach. Coming from Juba made that transition much easier for me. Juba was no joke. It is the post many people spend their entire careers trying to avoid, but I had put in my two years. In the internal logic of USAID bidding, surviving a high-risk, high-hardship post like South Sudan gives you a "golden ticket," a priority status that says: I did the hard time, now I get to choose where I want to go.

When the bid list came out, I looked at my options and only put down five countries this time, the minimum required. I knew I had a winning hand. I asked myself, Where is it hardest to get to? Where should I cash in my prize?

I didn't have the Spanish fluency needed for Latin America, the other "dream" region for USAID, so I turned my gaze back toward Asia. It was a choice between Thailand, Cambodia, and Vietnam. I even considered going back to the Philippines, this time as the Office Director, because I had loved my first two years there so much.

I did my research as usual. I called my old colleagues and spoke with those who had worked in Asia. Everyone loved Thailand more than any other place in the region.

I put my money on Thailand as number one, Cambodia as number two, and the Philippines as number three. I would have been happy with any of them.

When the assignment finally came through, and I saw "Thailand," I was super excited, yet I realized the timing wasn't perfect. I was turning fifty later in the year, and I would have a tiny window of time before I had to pack up for Bangkok after departing Juba.

I could've waited and celebrated overseas, but dragging everyone halfway around the world felt like a lot to ask. Plus, I would already be in transition around that time in the US, crashing at Nancy's place. I just wanted one last big moment with my people on this side of the planet before the next chapter officially started.

I started thinking about going to the Caribbean. It checked off all my preferred boxes: sun, heat, a beautiful ocean, and good food. I'd always wanted to see Barbados, Rihanna's home. The beaches looked like a dream, and honestly, it was a lot closer than Bangkok. So, I figured, why not make my fiftieth a farewell to my first half a century and a "hello" to the next one?

I started a group chat and invited anyone who was down. To my surprise, eighteen friends and cousins (Nancy included) signed up. We stayed at this great little hotel on the West Coast. I kept the itinerary loose, just color themes like "orange and blue day" or "purple pajama night" and let the group vibe take over.

We spent several days there touring the island, eating fresh flying fish and doubles, and swimming in water the color of gemstones. One day, we chartered a yacht with a DJ and danced barefoot in our all-white attire until the sun dropped. But the night of my actual birthday was the one that remains most memorable.

The hotel set up a white canvas tent right on the sand, so close to the water that the tide almost touched the flowing tablecloth. A soft breeze moved through, lifting the edges and cooling our bare feet. Everyone wore black, per my request.

I was mesmerized by our collective beauty as I looked at our group around the U-shaped table. Most were the same girls I'd grown up with in Queens. Forty years had passed, yet here we were, still choosing each other. Some came from far away, like my sister-friend Naomi, who traveled from Tanzania. Others I met later in life at work, like Aleathea and Toniqua. Doctors, senior directors and administrators, teachers, nurses, and journalists. Strong, passionate, driven women who had lived full lives and still showed up for mine.

As the sky softened into that brief, gentle blue before the orange sunset took over, drinks passed, and my friends argued, in the exact same New York accents we'd had since fourteen or so, about who would speak first. Monique, our resident songstress and dancer from Brooklyn, said something funny, and then my cousin Flo's cackle took us all out. We couldn't stop laughing, tears overflowing. Then, one by one, they came behind my chair, rested a hand on my shoulder, and spoke.

They remembered hopscotch in the street, first heartbreaks, evenings we dragged each other to parties. They talked about the harder years, too, divorces, sick parents, jobs that didn't work out, the times we held each other up without making a big deal of it. They said they were proud of me. They said my life had inspired them. That part touched me deeply.

One after another, they kept calling me "adventurous and brave." It made me laugh through the tears because, in my head, I am the least adventurous person I know. I'm the woman who would never, ever bungee jump or go rock climbing. I won't even hold a lizard if you paid me. To me, "adventure" sounds like something for people who like adrenaline and reptiles, and that's just not the kid.

But they weren't talking about bungee cords. They were talking about the version of me they'd watched for years: the girl from Queens with big dreams who actually went out and chased them. They saw the bravery in the moves I made, even when I just felt like I was only putting one foot in front of the other. And honestly? Listening to them, I realized they might have been on to something.

Yes, they were right, actually, because a week later, there I was, leaving for Thailand, on to the next adventure.

I thought I was ready for Bangkok. I'd lived in the Philippines before, so I figured I knew the drill. Another big Asian city, right? Hmph! Boy, was I wrong.

The second I stepped out of Suvarnabhumi Airport and looked up at the highway signs, I panicked. Every single one was in Thai script. No English translations in sight. My first thought was: How on earth would I ever be able to drive here? I'm somewhat of an undercover petrolhead. I like being behind the wheel, but looking at that chaotic traffic and the foreign signs, I immediately made a life-altering decision: I am not getting a car. I won't survive.

There is an overabundance of everything in Bangkok, including motor vehicles. People everywhere, tourists walking up and down, tuk-tuks zipping in and out of lanes, motorcycles pushing you aside on sidewalks, street food vendors on every corner, and shops that stay open 24/7. Never mind New York, Bangkok is truly the city that never sleeps.

The adjustment wasn't just about the streets; it was about my space. I hadn't lived in an apartment since grad school. In all my previous posts, except for Juba, where there was no choice, and back home, I had a house. Suddenly, I was downsizing into a high-rise. At first, I wasn't in love with it. It felt crammed and overwhelming. But with time, my perspective shifted. I began to enjoy the view, which offered an amazing sunset almost daily. I was surrounded by a lush park with a lake and water fountains, sleek skyscrapers, shopping malls, rooftop bars, and hospitals that looked like five-star hotels, complete with concierge desks and fresh orchids.

But the biggest shock wasn't the luxury; it was the rhythm. As a New Yorker, I'm wired to move fast. For the first month, I caught myself practically sprinting past people. I'd be thinking, *why are they walking so slowly? Is no one in a hurry?* But in Thailand, there's this "Zen-like" calm. People don't yell in the street. They don't even honk their horns in that gridlock traffic. Slowly, without me even noticing, Bangkok retrained my nervous system. I stopped rushing.

I started taking leisurely strolls, stopping at fruit stands to buy mangoes that rivaled those I had in the Philippines, along with my new favorites like dragon fruit and mangosteen. I walked to and from work as part of my daily routine, forty-plus minutes each way, wearing an extra layer of clothing to soak up my sweat. I learned to just walk behind people at their pace and allow the heat and humidity to hug me tightly.

Thai people are incredibly respectful and welcoming. They move with a softness that I came to rely on. Greetings came automatically, with a slight bow and a Y-hand gesture. Even the bustling city itself is super clean, despite the lack of trash cans; people just have this quiet discipline and pride.

The "weirdest" part for me? The safety. I could walk out at two in the morning, in pitch-black darkness, and nothing would happen. No one bothers you. No one stares, and no one is trying to mug you. To me, coming from the States, it felt almost unreal that a place this big and busy could be this safe. Until this day, I still couldn't tell you how this is possible.

Of course, nowhere is perfect. Through the embassy and USAID colleagues on other teams, I learned about the "darkness" near the borders, the scam compounds where people are lured with fake jobs and trafficked. Hearing those stories of hopeful people caught in something so awful, the "pig butchering" in this land of opulence and plenty, was one of the hardest things for me to comprehend while there.

But in and outside of the city, Thailand turned out to be exactly the kind of place I didn't know I needed. After the intensity of the last few years, like donning bulletproof vests just to visit clinics, this girl from Queens finally found a place where she could slow down, stop looking constantly over her shoulder, and just be.

My first week in the office, I found my deputy, Ben, who arrived in the country shortly before I did. We had met briefly in D.C., and seeing him again felt reassuring. He was incredibly supportive; by the time I arrived, he'd already handled so much of the groundwork. As time went on, he became a steady anchor I could count on, especially when I had to travel.

There's a specific kind of peace that comes with working in a place like Bangkok. Ben and I used to joke that if we both went down with food poisoning, our health team would keep humming along perfectly. Working with colleagues like Maprang and Panus was a dream. The Thai staff were meticulous and professional. No bullets flying overhead, no families living across borders in refugee camps like in Juba. People went home to their own homes and to their immediate families, and that stability meant they always brought their full selves to the office.

The team was almost entirely Thai, which put me in the minority again, a feeling I was now used to. I quickly realized that office life here had its own "Zen" rhythm. No one raised their voice; they were polite and quietly confident. Disagreements were handled in private with careful phrasing and long pauses. It took me a minute to realize that silence didn't mean they necessarily agreed with me; it meant they were choosing their words very, very carefully.

The work itself was a massive shift. In Africa, my focus was often on the general population, mothers, babies, and adolescent girls. In Thailand, an upper-middle-income country, the government actually covers about 95% of the population's health needs, which is extremely impressive. But it doesn't fully address the unique requirements of a very specific, niche population: the LGBTQI+ community. Even in a place as seemingly tolerant as Thailand, stigma and discrimination from public healthcare workers still exist. That's where USAID stepped in. The challenges here weren't about survival; there were no empty drug shelves or power outages like in Lesotho. Instead, the challenge was: How do you make a strong system even more equitable?

I started going out on day and night outreach visits with our local partners, and it was nothing like the hushed, anonymous services I'd seen elsewhere. We'd go to "walking streets" lined with bars, and our partners would set up bright tents with music and a game-show vibe. They'd run trivia games, and if you got the answer right, you'd win a pack of condoms or a voucher for the clinic.

They even had testing booths right there on the sidewalk. I was amazed at how open it was; people were laughing, flirting, and waiting in line like they were going to a nightclub, but instead it was for HIV tests, like it was the most natural thing in the world. And it worked. We were reaching the right segment of the population and getting HIV rates under control.

Our work with five local partners - SWING, IHRI, Caremat, Mplus, and RSAT - was one of the clearest examples of what sustainability can actually look like. With USAID support, each organization strengthened its technical, managerial, and operational capacity, moving beyond project-by-project survival to confidently providing technical assistance across the region. They were no longer just implementers, but regional leaders and global role models, training others, shaping best practices, and standing firmly in their own expertise. Watching that shift unfold felt deeply affirming; it was proof that we were on a real path toward sustainability, building something designed to last well beyond our direct involvement.

While the HIV work was creative and innovative, malaria was a more challenging puzzle. We were focused on the borders with Myanmar, where active conflict was pushing new cases into areas that hadn't budgeted for them. This, unfortunately, thwarted Thailand's claim to have eliminated malaria, a coveted public health status once imminent. Then there was Global Health Security, grappling with the legacy of COVID and adding anthrax and bird flu to the mix. For the first time in my career, I had brilliant veterinarians like Karoon and Palm on my team. I traveled and learned more about chickens, bats, and wet markets in my first year than I ever thought possible.

Whether it was work travel or personal, it was a relief to escape the thick air of Bangkok, where pollution could climb into extremely unhealthy levels, and to step beyond the city into places where I could finally breathe freely and move without a face mask. Thailand rewarded every mile traveled with beauty in a different way. In Koh Samui and Rayong, palm-lined beaches and slow, salt-soft mornings offered a gentler rhythm, where the sea seemed to quiet everything inside me. Ayutthaya unfolded in sun-bleached ruins and towering Buddha heads wrapped in roots, a powerful reminder of impermanence and time.

Up north in Chiang Mai, the air cooled, mountains rose, and temples glowed at dusk, grounding me in calm and reflection. Phuket pulsed with color and contrast, old town charm, dramatic coastlines, and water that shifted from turquoise to deep blue by the hour. And then there was the magic of island hopping: laughing macaques and postcard chaos at Monkey Island, followed by the unreal stillness of Maya Beach, where limestone cliffs cradle a lagoon so clear it hardly feels real. Each place offered its own lesson, history, joy, humility, wonder, and together they reminded me how vast and generous the world can be when you step outside routine and let the world meet you where you are.

Because Bangkok served as a regional hub, my team and I also spent much of our time hopping across Southeast Asia and the Pacific to provide technical assistance and fill gaps. I felt like I had won the lottery when I was asked to support our new Mission in Fiji. When I arrived in Suva, I worked with indigenous Fijians whose beautiful Afros and golden brown skin made me feel right at home, and by the end of day one, everyone was calling me their sister. It felt good to mentor this new team, who were eager to make a difference in their communities.

A few months later, I was sent to Samoa as the sole USAID representative for a WHO ministerial meeting. I spent a week in Apia, sitting at long negotiating tables with CDC colleagues, hashing out disease targets and policy commitments against a backdrop of black volcanic cliffs and a crashing sea. It was rugged and beautiful, and I promised myself I'd come back one day to explore without the badge and the agenda.

Then, right before Christmas, I got a call from the Philippines. They actually asked me *IF* I'd be interested in coming over for a couple of weeks to help out, as *IF* that was a real question. A chance to go back to my first post? I was on the next thing smoking, and I took Anthony with me. We were both high on nostalgia. Walking back into that office was like pressing play on an old tape. The same guards waved hello; the same view of Manila Bay stared back at me. My old staff hugged me like I'd just stepped out for coffee instead of being gone for over a decade.

All in all, it was serious, soul-stretching work. And before I even realized how much time had passed, I hit my second year in Bangkok. Looking back at that journey from the "Jen at 50" tent in Barbados to this 26th-floor view, it all felt validated when the news came through: I had been promoted from my current personal grade to the next one up. It was the perfect "period" at the end of this chapter, something I had been praying for, ten years and counting. The girl from Queens was finally thriving.

But even in that stability, I was navigating a landscape that didn't always have a "mirror" for me.

Most of my fellow USAID directors were more senior in rank because Bangkok is such a "prize" post; the competition was high. Externally, I was almost always the only Black person in the room.

Once, someone confided in me that before a high-level technical meeting with the Ministry of Health, a team member suggested, very carefully, *"Maybe we should invite the Mission Director instead."* They wondered if the audience would respond better to a different face, which was code for race. They thought there would be more "automatic" credibility if a white face showed up instead of mine. No one ever questioned my authority directly, but that hesitation lingered.

It was a subtle reminder that for women of color in spaces where we are in the minority, competence is rarely enough. You can be the director, you can be the most prepared person in the room, and you still feel that silent pressure to prove you belong in a chair others are just presumed to own. Or you can do everything right, and then someone sabotages you, "accidentally," along the way. Like the time one of my supervisors gave me a less-than-stellar rating, claiming a case of mistaken identity. She said she had another colleague in mind when submitting my file. Like seriously. Who does that?

It was no wonder it had taken me a full decade to move one grade up along the scale. Ten years riddled with fits and starts. Meanwhile, I watched other colleagues, especially white men, cruise past that milestone in half the time, some hitting the highest rank while I was still clawing my way through. At the time, I didn't call it an injustice; I just put my head down and worked. But in all honesty, at times it felt like I was running a race with weights on my ankles that others didn't have to wear.

But despite the "only-ness," the slow promotions, and some embassy politics I will not bore you with, I never lost sight of my long-term goals.

Then, a bridge collapsed.

It was January 20, 2025.

Late Monday night, my phone started buzzing like crazy while I was at home in my Bangkok apartment as the Martin Luther King, Jr. holiday wrapped up on my side of the world. I checked my messages, and there were several links to the White House's website for:

"Executive Order 14169, Reevaluating and Realigning United States Foreign Aid"

"Executive Order 14151, Ending Radical and Wasteful Government DEI Programs and Preferencing"

"Executive Order 14155, Withdrawing the United States from the World Health Organization"

Group chats from every corner of the USAID world, from D.C. to Juba to Pretoria, were exploding. It was pure chaos. I was answering frantic texts from relatives worried about my paycheck, friends confused by the news, and contractors who wanted to know whether their programs were being shuttered effective immediately.

Holy sh*t, I thought. What in the world is happening? If this were day one of the new Trump administration, what would the next 1,460 days look like? Honestly, deep down, I kept waiting for the "adults" to enter the room. Surely Congress will stop this madness, I told myself, or some high-level judge will advise them accordingly. They'll explain that you can't just erase sixty-plus years of diplomacy and development with a keystroke. It can't be done.

I was wrong. We were all wrong.

An email from our Mission Director came in, addressed to all Senior Staff: "Subject: 8 am Emergency Session: Review of Executive Orders."

We were summoned to meet first thing in the morning. When I walked into the office that morning, the "Zen" was gone. Everyone walked into the conference room looking like zombies, as if still in a daze from the news that finally made its way to us from Washington. We were told that all non-essential activities had to be paused with immediate effect, and we were to have no contact with external stakeholders until further notice.

Excuse me? How could this be? My team and I were in the midst of organizing a high-level delegation from Washington to attend the largest annual Thai health convening, the Prince Mahidol Award Conference. I had spent months on working committees with Thai counterparts planning for this. I was also just on the cusp of launching our inaugural Regional Health Donors Coordination Committee with French Embassy counterparts as co-leads. And just like that, we had to ghost all of them. I have never been so professionally embarrassed in my life.

My team was staring at their screens glass-eyed. We had gone from planning the next decade of health security to wondering if our keycards would still work by lunchtime. It was heartbreaking to watch a legacy being dismantled by people who have never set foot in the communities we served. The "next chapter" wasn't just swallowing us up. It was being rewritten by someone else entirely with an abrupt ending.

The following week, hundreds of contractors were let go from our Washington Office, just like that. Friends and colleagues, some who had been working for the agency for a decade or more, were shockingly terminated with immediate effect. Then, a few days later, our agency website went dark. Gone, just like that. And just when we thought it couldn't get any worse, our own government turned on us and called us names and demonized our work.

"Radical left lunatics." "Evil, criminal organization." "Tremendous fraud, waste, and abuse."

Again, I was shocked. Who and what were they talking about? I was so confused and angry. In every country I worked in, I labored alongside dedicated men and women of all nationalities who were doing their best to improve the lives of the clients we served. I had no idea what the White House was accusing us of then, and I still don't know now.

The next couple of weeks were spent in twice-daily huddle meetings trying to make sense of everything and figure out the best way forward. I tried my best to keep a straight face and a strong demeanor for my team's sake, doing my best to keep morale up as much as possible.

Meanwhile, I was also thinking of home because I was missing my mom's birthday. She's a Valentine baby.

Given the extraordinary situation at the office, I decided not to go back for it. My mom's dementia had left her mostly non-verbal at that stage, so I couldn't just call her to wish her a happy birthday. I had to rely on Nancy to pass on the message when she went to visit. I just hoped to get a few pictures back from the facility staff that they took of her during the day.

I felt caught in the cruelest of intersections: between an agency that no longer valued my service and a mother who, in her fading memory, sometimes struggled to remember she even had a daughter.

I was at a crossroads, not sure which way I was going.

Bangkok 26th floor office.

Amazing temple in Chiang Mai, Thailand.

Celebrating my 50th birthday in Barbados with some of the crew in October 2023.

A joyful celebration for Mom's milestone 80th birthday with family.

Chapter Seventeen

THINGS FALL APART

"I didn't want to bother you, but Mom has been hospitalized. They say she has pneumonia."

This is the kind of communication that you dread when you are in the foreign service. An ailing parent in need when you are so far away. This was just a week and a half after Mom's birthday.

I felt guilty. There I was in Bangkok, worried about Executive Orders, while my sister was juggling a full-time job, taking care of my brother-in-law, and now hospital visits. I couldn't just stare at the screen. I tapped the call button immediately.

"Please, just don't worry," Nancy insisted. "I know you're busy with work. You probably couldn't get away even if you wanted to."

"Nancy, I just want to make sure…"

"I have it under control," she said firmly. "I'll keep you posted."

The line went dead. *Yeah, right*, I thought. She doesn't have this handled at all. I didn't text her back. Instead, I walked straight into the office.

"I'm sorry to do this," I told the team, "But I need to go home immediately."

Luckily, Ben, being the rockstar that he is, reassured me that if I needed to go to the US, he'd hold down the fort. That was all I needed to hear. I booked the next flight out and was on my way to Maryland.

I arrived at Bangkok International Airport, tightened my luggage handle, kept walking, and thought about the long ride ahead. I felt my phone pinging with emails streaming in. Whatever Washington was up to these days could wait one more layover. I was a daughter on my way home to relieve my sister and help care for my mom.

When I arrived, I went straight to the hospital. Nancy was already at her bedside. We weren't sure if she could hear us, or even register that we were there. Then, for a moment so quick we almost doubted it had happened, she opened her eyes. She looked at us and gave the faintest smile. For the first time, we felt she knew we were there. I was so relieved and happy.

In that moment, the 26th-floor office and the "Jen at 50" celebrations felt like they belonged to a different person. Here, in the silence of the ward, the only thing that mattered was the breath of the woman beside me. I could lose my agency, my title, and my certainty, but as I sat there with the woman who carried me, I realized I hadn't lost my soul.

I closed my eyes and, for the first time in weeks, I just took some deep breaths and prayed.

I ended up staying for two weeks, long enough to see small signs of improvement. I remember sitting beside her with a spoon of soft food, hoping she might wake up enough to take one bite. At times, I sat in silence with a book, looked up now and then, hoping my presence would help her recover. The doctor gave the good news that the pneumonia had cleared up, and she could go home. So I helped Nancy get Mom settled back into the facility, and the following day, I was back up in the air, going back to Bangkok.

I got back to the office and found things under control, yet the atmosphere was more tense. There were talks of more layoffs, including for folks like me, for everyone. No one knew exactly when, but we were told it could be imminent. Anxiety levels for myself and the whole mission were running high. Then we got the directive from Washington, "all staff except for essential personnel will be placed on Administrative Leave, and staff overseas are recalled back to the US, within 30 days."

More shock. 30 days? My 15-year USAID foreign service career was about to end without cause, just like that? Our union tried to reassure us that they'd help stop this craziness. There had to be due process since we had protections in place. This could only happen with an Act of Congress, they said. I hoped and prayed they were right.

Back in my Bangkok apartment, another evening, I got a phone call from Nancy. This time, she didn't attempt to sugarcoat it. "Mom is sick again, and this time it's not looking good. I think you should come home if you can."

If I can? This time I didn't ask permission. I just told Ben and my supervisor that I had to go. I booked my ticket and packed my bags.

Once again, I found myself racing around the world, caught in the hum of the cabin. I sat there doing the terrible math of which thread would snap: the one tying my mother to this world, or the one that held my identity to my work. And I knew, with a desperate clarity, that I would have traded everything to save them both.

I kept replaying that brief smile from February, hoping she might recognize me just once more. I needed her voice and her guidance. I needed a listener. But I knew the woman who could have helped was already gone; the last time I'd seen her, she had mistaken me for her own mother and tried to tip me for the drive home.

As I sat in the dark cabin, I practiced what I'd say when I finally reached her. I prayed for the strength to take her hand and say, "Mom, they're letting me go, and I don't know who I am without the work." I needed her to hear me, even if she forgot the words before I finished the sentence.

Then my phone buzzed while I was mid-air, having just left my layover in Doha, and now on the final leg to Washington. My heart lurched before I even saw the screen; in my life, a vibration at thirty thousand feet never brings good news. It was a message from Nancy.

I stared at the two words. They sat apart from each other. Mom's. Gone. I blinked, looked up at the reading light above, then down again. The letters hadn't changed.

A flight attendant paused by my row. "Can I get you anything?"

I looked at her. I saw her mouth move, heard the sound, but it was noise. I managed to shake my head. She smiled and moved down the aisle. The plane hummed on. Nothing had changed for anyone else but me.

I folded forward, the seatbelt pinning me to the chair as I collapsed into myself. A raw, choked groan escaped. Why didn't I leave a day earlier? Why wasn't I there? I shouldn't have gone back to Thailand in February. I should never have left her side. I sat there, doubled over, wondering who I was even supposed to be without her.

When the plane finally landed, my legs felt like water. I shuffled up the jet bridge, dragging my suitcase, the same one that had survived mortar fire in Juba and flash floods in Lesotho. Now, it just felt like it was full of bricks.

Nancy and Anthony were waiting under the Arrivals board, eyes puffy, arms already out. I went to my sister and rested my head on her shoulder. I wept so hard I felt like something inside me might actually break.

The drive home was quiet, save for the GPS lady's calm voice saying "recalculating" each time we missed a turn. None of us could see through the tears. The second we got home, the grieving stopped, and the logistics took over.

For the next forty-eight hours, we were funeral robots. We chose the casket material and color, debated carnations versus roses, and picked the photo that made Mom look most like herself. I can tell you, nothing prepares you for the task of choosing your mother's casket or what she'll wear inside of it.

On the third night, we sat at the dining room table surrounded by sympathy cards and old photo albums. Nancy and I had been out shopping all day, looking for black dresses and matching accessories. We were worn out. I remember thinking nothing else could happen that night.

And then, my work phone buzzed. I flipped it over, took a brief look, and didn't need to read any further. In fact, there was nothing much to read.

Reduction-in-Force. Effective September 2. Separation date final.

That was it. No "Dear," no "thank you," no signature. Just three lines that ended fifteen years of service. I read it out loud to the room. Nancy and Anthony just nodded. We were already so hollowed out by grief that the news slid in without a splash.

Anthony exhaled slowly, staring at his phone. He'd been quiet for a long time before he finally looked up. "Mom, you're never going to believe this," he said, his voice flat. "There was an earthquake. A huge one in Thailand." He turned the screen toward me.

The headline was blunt: Major Earthquake Near Mandalay in Myanmar. The tremors had rippled across the region, including Bangkok. I stared at the date: March 28, 2025. The same week of my mother's passing. The same date as the layoff notice I was still holding. I felt a hysterical laugh bubble up and die in my throat. Was this some cosmic joke? Here I was choosing my mother's casket, getting laid off, and on the same day learning that an actual earthquake had hit Bangkok.

It was too much. My mother was gone, my career was over, and the place where I lived was a disaster zone. I couldn't process it. Did I even have an apartment to go back to? I stood up without a word and went to my bedroom. I just needed the door to close.

Inside, the math started to eat at me. I was three years from full retirement. I had planned every post and every bid around finishing the full ride. Thailand was supposed to be my last stop before a stint in Washington. All those nights in malaria zones, the lonely Christmases, and the climb to senior leadership were just gone. I had never been laid off or failed an assignment. Now, I was being let go because someone in Washington decided my life's work was unnecessary. I sat up all night, holding mom's funeral program that was beautifully created by Stephanie in one hand and a layoff notice in the other, trying to figure out which death I was supposed to mourn first.

We had to wait a week and a half for the burial because the church we wanted was fully booked. Those ten days felt suspended. We answered calls, welcomed relatives I hadn't seen in decades, and moved through everything on autopilot.

When the service finally came, I listened as people spoke about my mother in ways I hadn't always considered. Hans talked about how she had helped repair his relationship with our father and convinced him to buy him a new car. Standing there, I realized that for all the years I'd focused on her flaws, I had overlooked the reach of her impact. She had shaped lives in ways I never fully saw.

People are always larger than the version we carry in our heads. My mom certainly was.

I stayed in Maryland for a month to help Nancy get things in order. I never realized how much of a job it is when someone dies. My days were spent on the phone canceling subscriptions, sitting in bank offices, and signing my name on what felt like a thousand different forms.

My sister and I went through my mom's belongings at the care facility, figuring out what to keep and what to donate. Every time we taped a box shut, it felt like we were checking off another part of her life. But eventually, there were no more boxes to pack and no more forms to sign. I had to face my return flight. I packed my own bags to go back to a job that had already fired me and a life that no longer existed. This time, I had Anthony go back with me. I needed the support.

I think I'd hoped the funeral would help me bury everything at once. I wanted to believe that if we put my mother in the ground, my career and my anxiety would go down with her. But I learned that no coffin is big enough to hold that much loss. Some things you can't just bury; you have to carry them back with you.

As Anthony and I left that morning, my sister and I shared a long, wordless hug in the doorway. Her arms were the closest thing I had left to a home. Getting into the taxicab felt like a cruel rehearsal. I wasn't going back to my life; I was heading back to Bangkok to pack it into boxes. I would eventually return to a country where my mother was buried, and my job was gone. What is home without my mother?

Flying back felt like returning to a disaster zone, but the disaster was mine as much as the city's. The news was showing collapsed buildings and families afraid to sleep in their homes. I thought seeing that kind of loss might make my own grief feel smaller, but it didn't. It just made everything feel heavier.

Then we walked into my apartment.

I knew right away I had to leave. The earthquake had hit the place hard. There were fine, jagged cracks running down the walls in several rooms, and paint chips were scattered over the floor like freckles. A long crack even ran right behind my bed headboard. I didn't feel safe.

The embassy moved us to a hotel for ten days while they checked the building. When the assessment came back, they told me the structure was sound enough, and the cracks would be fixed only after we moved out. We had to go back. We lived in that cracked house and prayed there wouldn't be another tremor to finish what the first one had started.

Being back in the apartment only made it harder to keep things together. I tried to stay composed, but the smallest things would set me off. I had photos of my mom everywhere, a whole wall of us over the years. I'd walk past and see her smiling beside my son when he was four and then again when he was twenty. Her face warmed me and broke me at the same time. I'd look at her and realize I'd never see her like that again in the flesh.

I didn't feel like myself, and I definitely didn't have the energy to pretend I was okay.

I requested a few more weeks off from work to breathe, but I was told it wasn't possible. With the layoffs and all the uncertainty, the expectation was that I needed to be there to lead the team through the transition. The irony was that there wasn't much left to lead. Our partners were grounded, and the staff were mostly just sitting there, waiting for the next blow. There wasn't necessarily a crisis to solve, but the system wanted a leader in the chair to make the collapse look orderly.

I went back because I felt I had no choice. My job still demanded more of me, and yet I was standing there empty, with practically nothing left to give.

During the day, I was the "captain on deck," talking about transitions and projecting a calm I didn't feel internally. Then I'd go home and watch six Thai movers wrap my life in brown paper. The men walked through the rooms with rolls of tape and blank boxes. In a few hours, my clothes, my books, and my son's drawings all disappeared into cardboard.

As the furniture disappeared, the cracks in the walls became impossible to ignore. Without my things to distract me, I was left with the damage. I'd stand in a half-empty room and realize I was boxing up fifteen years for a destination I hadn't even chosen yet. I felt a little foolish worrying about whether I had enough clothes to survive the next two weeks.

In the middle of all this, I was also carrying the weight of the programs we were dropping. It wasn't just disheartening; it was embarrassing. We had made promises to people, told them we'd walk with them. I committed to never looking away. And then overnight, we pulled the rug from under them.

It was humiliating to watch the news and see politicians ranting about "mismanagement." They made us look like criminals, ignoring the decades of work and audits that actually built those systems. They didn't see or care about the refugee families who relied on us for food or the HIV patients who needed those supply chains to stay alive. To the politicians, it was a line item to cut and a headline to brag about, but to us, it was a daily shame.

I felt a strange relief to be in Thailand, where the government could absorb the hit, but I couldn't stop thinking about my colleagues in places like South Sudan or Tanzania. In some countries, our funding was the only thing keeping clinics open. I heard stories of patients left stranded and systems collapsing overnight because no one could fill the funding gap.

Kate, my Irish-American colleague in the Thailand office, gave us a moment none of us were prepared for, and one we will never forget. In the middle of our final days, as the office was winding down and the weight of the inevitable pressed in on all of us, she lifted her violin and began to play, right there among our desks and half-packed boxes. Thai and American colleagues quietly gathered around, drawn in by the music's softness and sorrow, holding back tears as the notes filled the space where so much shared purpose, late nights, and hard-won progress had once lived. In that fragile, suspended moment, we weren't policymakers or professionals trying to make sense of a shifting world; we were simply human, grieving the end of a chapter and coming to terms with the truth that, despite our best efforts and our belief that we were doing the right things, our lives would never be the same again.

What helped me get through my last days in Bangkok were the farewells. I had a Japanese dinner with Ayana, my old Scrabble rival, and Kyra, our steady hand. Cassandre was there too, my Haitian-American sister, and she looked at me across the table and said, "You've survived a lot worse than a move. Don't forget who you are when you get to Maryland. You're still the woman who ran those programs."

Then there was lunch with Jane, my friend Desta's mom, at one of our favorite restaurants in the EmQuartier Mall. I found comfort in spending time with her, as if she were my mom, too. She held my hand across the table for a long time. When I tried to apologize for being such a mess, she just squeezed my fingers. "Don't you dare apologize," she whispered. "You're mourning a mother and a life at the same time. You just sit here and breathe."

Every goodbye felt like tearing something away that had only just started to take root. When people asked what I would miss, I gave them the easy answers: the safety, the weather, the street food. But the real answer was that I was being forced back to a place that hadn't been home for practically two decades. I was going back to a townhouse I'd walked out of fifteen years ago, to a country where the person who brought me into this world was buried in Maryland soil.

The story here was ending mid-sentence. I was headed for a new chapter where the most important character was gone.

On my last morning, I stood in the empty living room with my suitcases at my feet. The place was completely quiet, and even my own breathing seemed too loud. My eyes drifted to the crack behind where my bed used to be.

For weeks, I'd been convinced the ceiling would drop on me. But it hadn't. The building had held, and so had I.

I said a quiet goodbye to the walls and the woman I'd spent over twenty-five years becoming. There was no plan. It was just me and whatever came next.

That "whatever" was a terrifying blank space. For decades, I'd measured my life in assignments and cables. Now, for the first time, I didn't have a post or a mission to move onto. I was middle-aged and starting from ground zero.

But as I reached for the handle of my suitcase, I felt something small and stubborn in my chest. It wasn't hope. Hope feels too bright for a moment like this. It was just the plain fact that I was still standing, and it was time to move on.

The ground had shaken, the walls had cracked, and everything I'd counted on had slipped away, yet I was still breathing.

Anthony stepped out into the hallway with our bags and pressed the elevator button. I took one last look at the bare rooms and that scar on the wall. I pulled the door shut and walked out without looking back.

I was still here. And I was still moving forward.

Things were falling apart, in the words of Chinua Achebe, but I wondered, were they actually falling into place?

Mom celebrating her birthday at her care facility in Maryland.

With Anthony and Nancy at Dulles airport.

Anthony all grown up!

Conclusion

FROM QUEENS TO THE WORLD

Much of my life has unfolded as a series of things falling apart. A career disrupted. Identities questioned. Families reshaped by maladies and time. I carry this cycle of collapse and rebirth in my bones, passed down from my Haitian parents who left behind everything they knew to build a life from scratch in New York.

I never intended to travel the world for a living or become a diplomat. My initial plan was to become a pediatrician, but later that shifted to dreams of Broadway and Hollywood. Immigrant life in Queens offered many things, but not an acting scholarship, and my mother was not interested in dreams of fame.

"Be realistic," my mom always told me.

I swapped my acting ambitions for what I believed was a more practical escape. I exchanged the stage for the classroom and the spotlight for public service. I became an "accidental" diplomat, representing a government I wanted to believe in, even when it meant setting aside my own views and embracing a mission that was not always my own.

When I began my role as a Peace Corps volunteer in 1999, the world faced seemingly insurmountable challenges. Communities were devastated by HIV and AIDS, particularly among young people in southern Africa. Diseases such as tuberculosis remained a constant threat. Gender-based violence was widespread, often unreported, and constituted a silent epidemic that required urgent action.

Over the years, I saw real progress across many countries. HIV infection rates declined in many places due to increased awareness and improved access to treatment. Tuberculosis and malaria prevention efforts saved lives. Gender-based violence became more widely recognized and addressed, with many countries implementing stricter laws and support systems for survivors. Women's rights and education advanced as we addressed deep inequities, capping off over two decades of work rooted in partnership, patience, and a belief in people.

Providing foreign assistance was never just a job. It was a calling. This work gave my life meaning and connected me to an extended family of colleagues, friends, and communities across continents.

Then, in a single moment, it all vanished. A single executive order stripped away our roles, our identities, and our purpose. With that stroke of a black Sharpie pen, the administration shut down programs, erased agencies, and put lives at risk. To the world, those folks in Washington might have made headlines; to us, their names marked the end of our careers, crushing our aspirations, silencing years of progress, and abandoning communities worldwide. It still feels like the greatest betrayal, not just to us as foreign aid workers but more importantly to the people we served.

They didn't just cancel programs; they tore down the entire machinery overnight. They threw out local staff and diplomats without a word of warning or a shred of respect.

That moment wasn't just political; it was personal and

communal. What most people don't see is that aid isn't only about budget spreadsheets or fancy receptions; it's about lifelines. HIV clinics lost support staff, and with them, the ability to keep patients on life-saving treatment. Maternal and child health programs, which had cut infant mortality rates, were gutted overnight.

I thought of the young woman in Lesotho who told me the clinic was the reason she was still alive. What would she do when her pills and injections ran out?

Gender-based violence programs were among the first to fall because most sat under the DEI umbrella. Survivors who finally had a shelter or an advocate slid back into silence, returning to a world that told them once again they were on their own. I thought of the 12-year-old girl in Tanzania who stayed in school because we covered her tuition, or the village that had just learned to irrigate its crops and produce more nutritious foods for the orphans.

Cuts like these don't just end projects; they kill people. They erase stories and hollow out momentum. They force communities to relearn despair. What people often miss is that foreign assistance isn't charity. It's empowerment and infrastructure, education and medication, training and advocacy. It is dignity and hope.

Even with that belief, I do not hold rose-colored views about foreign assistance. No system is perfect. I saw inefficiencies, misaligned incentives, and moments when donor priorities overshadowed local leadership. But those never outweighed the good.

I believe the future of development must hand responsibility and decision-making power back to recipient governments and communities. Sustainable progress requires increased domestic investment, stronger accountability to citizens, and partnerships that extend beyond traditional donors to include the private sector, philanthropy, social enterprises, and other nontraditional actors. Foreign assistance should be catalytic, not permanent. It should help countries build the capacity and confidence to stand on their own, on their own terms.

Yes, it was painful when our work at USAID ended so abruptly. I am still holding onto the grief, not just for myself but for the hundreds of thousands of lives affected. I have been traumatized. So many people have been traumatized all over the world. For those of us who intertwined our identities with this work, losing it felt like losing a part of ourselves. We fought a lifetime to find our purpose, only to see it dismantled overnight by politics, not by war or disease. The deepest pain isn't just what I lost; it's what the world lost.

Yet, I am certain that this part of my journey achieved its purpose. The impact lives on through children who still remember a lesson, communities where the seeds of change continue to sprout, and friendships that still span borders. I have seen people rise, adapt, find new ways to continue their work, and keep their dreams alive. I have sat in South African township classrooms where children learned to write their names on chalkboards that barely stood, yet they went on to become successful contributors to their communities. I have seen women in Lesotho pooling their coins to buy one bag of maize so no family goes hungry that night. I have watched youth in Dar es Salaam and Juba turn music, art, and sport into movements of resistance and pride. In Thailand and the Philippines, it was impressive and inspiring to see development look less like rescue and more like true partnerships, with governments increasingly positioned to lead.

If there is one truth I carry forward, it is this: the human spirit bends but does not break, no matter how often the ground shifts. That is why service continues even when institutions crumble. The end of a program cannot erase the people it touched. Peace, love, resilience, and restoration will always prevail.

The most difficult territory I ever had to navigate wasn't a foreign country. It was my own life.

Living this life of service didn't grant me immunity from pain. I learned to hold joy and heartbreak together, with victories in one hand and losses in the other. I had to learn to navigate different cultures and customs, often far from home. My marriage ended shortly after it began, forcing me to rebuild my life while caring for my son. I became a single parent, facing lonely nights and the intricate challenges of raising my child across different countries.

In my professional life, I faced discrimination that was sometimes subtle and sometimes blatant in environments where I was already a minority. My body also bore an accumulation of fractures and tears that eventually necessitated surgeries and left me with chronic pain.

The deepest cost, however, was grief layered over time. Dementia slowly stole the woman who anchored my life. I had to carry the hard truth of her decline while serving abroad, watching her fade both in person and from a distance. Losing her without a final goodbye remains an open wound, but I also carry the quiet sorrow of losing her twice: first to the disease and finally to death.

Alongside that grief, I carry unanswered questions about what constant relocation may have taken from my son, even as it strengthened him in ways I am still learning to understand. I often wonder how much stability he truly lost, or if those shifts made him all the more resilient and brilliant.

To those who dream of a life dedicated to service, who seek a purpose, and who wish to make an impact, do not fear this path. It will cost you. You may lose sleep, comfort, and even relationships. Yet what you gain is far greater: the chance to experience the world as an active participant, not just a tourist; the opportunity to touch lives and be transformed by them. Welcome the journey.

The Diplomat Queens Made isn't about geography but about possibility. It is proof that someone like me, who started in the most unlikely of places, can still make a difference at home and across oceans.

In the end, my story of becoming isn't about titles or positions; it's about choosing a life of service. "The World in My Bones" isn't just the title of my story. It's the path I walked. It began on a quiet street in Queens with a child who dreamed of escape, and carried me to places I never even imagined. What I thought was a career became a calling. What I thought was giving turned out to be receiving. And what I thought would be a straight climb forward became a winding road of laughter and tears, victories and losses, loneliness and belonging.

I am back home in the US, navigating resettlement and reverse culture shock. I'm no longer just the girl who wanted to escape, nor just the woman tethered to a government mission. I am both and everything in between. I am an immigrant child who fought for her place in the world and a diplomat who has conquered paths she never imagined. Although service cost me dearly, I would choose it again because my cup has refilled time after time.

I'm embracing this moment to explore other passions, including more travel, the arts and culture, storytelling, philanthropy, and wellness. I'm starting again, but I carry with me the certainty that beginnings arise from endings, and my story isn't over yet.

I am not a monolith, and I don't want to live inside anyone else's boxes anymore. I want to color outside the lines. I want to do ten things at once or none. I want to follow my heart and find joy continuously. I want to follow the road that feels most true, even when it is not the straightest. I want love. I want freedom. I want peace.

And as I continue to search for meaning in this collapse, I return to Chinua Achebe's classic *Things Fall Apart*. Achebe reminds us that collapse is not the end of the story; it is the moment when illusions fall away, and truth becomes unavoidable.

When things fall apart, we finally see what holds them together, and what never truly was.

If you are reading this at a moment when your life feels uncertain or undone, know that falling apart does not mean you have failed. See it as an invitation to rebuild with more truth. Honor where you come from, even as you step into what comes next. Trust what your bones already know. Becoming is not a destination. It is a lifelong practice.

Thank you for walking with me to this point. The story continues, for both of us.

Our last family portrait wearing the same colors.

Third-grade class picture in St Claire, Rosedale, New York.

Final year of middle school with Shel and Lazette in Hollis, Queens.

ACKNOWLEDGEMENTS

First and always, for my mother, Ginette, our *Gin Gin*. Your strength, devotion, and sacrifices shaped every chapter of my life, long before I ever put pen to paper. No matter where the journey of time takes us, your love has been my compass. This book exists because of you.

To my son Anthony, your kindness, creativity, and unconditional love mean everything to me. I love you more than I can explain. Infinite love to my sister Nancy, who is my rock, my biggest cheerleader, and my personal guardian angel. Heartfelt thanks to my extended family and friends for your constant encouragement and support.

My sincere appreciation to my mentors, colleagues, and friends across the world. Your wisdom, generosity, and shared purpose have profoundly shaped my journey. Special thanks to my editor, Maria MacAndrew, and to the early beta readers and literary supporters who walked this manuscript with me. Your thoughtful feedback, honesty, and care strengthened both the story and the storyteller.

Finally, to my readers: thank you for joining me on this journey of vulnerability and transparency. Thank you for trusting my voice and for carrying these stories forward. May my story inspire you to embrace your own unexpected paths and to live meaningfully, laugh heartily, and love boldly. Big hugs!

Touring Harare and taking in the views.

A circle of friends, including Veronica, in Zimbabwe, 1993.

ABOUT THE AUTHOR

Jennifer Erie, also known as 'Fête Jen,' is a seasoned international development professional, diplomat, creative entrepreneur, and passionate cultural ambassador. Born and raised in Queens, New York, to Haitian immigrant parents, Jennifer has spent more than two decades in public service, health, community development, and the transformative power of the creative arts.

As a Foreign Service Officer with the United States Agency for International Development (USAID) for over 15 years, Jennifer has led significant global health programs across Africa, Asia, and the Pacific Islands, focusing on HIV/AIDS, maternal and child health, global health security, malaria, gender-based violence, youth empowerment, and mental health. Her tenure at USAID included assignments in South Sudan, Tanzania, Thailand, the Philippines, Papua New Guinea, and Southern Africa, where she integrated public health strategies with innovative cultural platforms to amplify the voices of marginalized communities and promote human dignity.

Beyond her diplomatic endeavors, Jennifer is an accomplished creative arts producer and philanthropist through her Fête Jen enterprise. She established performing arts platforms that support emerging artists in Tanzania and the region. She manages talent in the creative industries and produces literary pieces, songs, and music videos. This unique enterprise combines her love for storytelling, international travel, cultural retreats, arts programming, talent management, social impact, and philanthropy advising. Inspired by her Haitian heritage and the resilient spirit of her late mother, Ginette, she is also developing Feròs, a lifestyle brand celebrating strength, elegance, and legacy. Feròs is the sister brand of Fierce, run by her beloved son, Anthony Kagiso Mboyane.

Jennifer holds a master's degree from American University and a bachelor's degree from Syracuse University. She began her international journey as a study abroad student in Zimbabwe in the early 1990s, later serving as a Peace Corps Volunteer in South Africa. These formative experiences laid the groundwork for a later career as a U.S. diplomat and Foreign Service Officer with USAID.

Her personal experiences navigating complex cultural dynamics, career transitions, and family legacies form the heart of her memoir, "The World in My Bones: The Diplomat Queens Made." Through her storytelling, she seeks to inspire others to embrace unexpected paths, celebrate cultural connections, and pursue transformative impact.

Jennifer currently resides in the U.S., continuing her journey as a global citizen, grounded in creative expression, holistic wellness, and a deep commitment to service. She can be reached at fetejen@gmail.com.